HOLY GHOST
IS *My* FRIEND

**A GREAT FRIEND WHO MUST
NEVER BE IGNORED AGAIN**

HOLY GHOST
IS *My* FRIEND

A GREAT FRIEND WHO MUST
NEVER BE IGNORED AGAIN

A Gift From God

WELLINGTON BOONE

APPTE Publishing
Norcross, Georgia
"We Publish the Fivefold"

The following abbreviations are used to identify
versions of the Bible used in this book:

KJV *King James Version,* also known as the *Authorized Version.* (Public domain)

NASB. Scripture quotations taken from the New American Standard Bible®,
Copyright © 1960, 1962, 1963, 1968, 1971, 1972, 1973,
1975, 1977, 1995 by The Lockman Foundation
Used by permission. (www.Lockman.org)

NKJV Scripture taken from the New King James Version®.
Copyright © 1982 by Thomas Nelson, Inc. Used by permission. All rights reserved.

NLT Scripture quotations marked NLT are taken from the Holy Bible, New Living
Translation, copyright © 1996, 2004, 2007 by Tyndale House Foundation. Used by
permission of Tyndale House Publishers, Inc., Carol Stream, Illinois 60188. All
rights reserved. New Living, NLT, and the New Living Translation logo are
registered trademarks of
Tyndale House Publishers.

Nouns and pronouns referring to deity are capitalized throughout the
text of this book unless they are included within a direct quotation,
in which case the original capitalization is retained.

Printed in the United States of America
December 2011

ISBN-10: 0984782109
ISBN-13: 9780984782109

Library of Congress Control Number: 2011962231

PUBLISHED BY APPTE PUBLISHING
5875 Peachtree Industrial Blvd. Suite 300
Norcross, GA 30092

770-840-0888

http://shop.apptepublishing.com

CONTENTS

SECTION 1—HOLY GHOST HIGHLIGHTS

SECTION 2—HOLY GHOST AND JESUS

SECTION 3—HOLY GHOST FRIENDSHIP AND YOU

APPENDICES

SECTION 1.
HOLY GHOST HIGHLIGHTS

HOLY GHOST WAS THERE!

- Creation
- Great Old Testament Revivals
- All Prophets and Prophecies Were Holy Ghost Work
- Conception of Jesus
- Baptism of Jesus
- Acknowledgement of Public Call By Jesus
- Led Jesus into the Wilderness to Be Tempted by the Devil
- Anointed Jesus with Power in Public Ministry
- Raised Jesus from the Dead
- Came to the Disciples at Pentecost
- Acts of the Apostles Are Acts of the Holy Ghost

And many more . . .

1

MY FRIEND IN
HIGH PLACES

*"Greater love hath no man than this,
that a man lay down his life for his friends."*[1]

*"The high and lofty one who lives in eternity,
the Holy One, says this:
'I live in the high and holy place with those
whose spirits are contrite and humble.
I restore the crushed spirit of the humble and
revive the courage of
those with repentant hearts.'"*[2]

In John 15, Jesus made a startling announcement to His disciples. He said that from now on He would call His disciples His friends. Friendship would now characterize His relationship with His followers, not a master/servant relationship.

> *"Henceforth I call you not servants; for the servant knoweth not what his lord doeth: but I have called you friends."*[3]

---

[1] John 15:13 KJV.
[2] Isaiah 57:15 NLT.
[3] John 15:15 KJV.

In fact, Jesus promised His disciples an *extreme* friendship where He would expose to them all of the secret things that He had heard from His Father.

> *". . . for all things that I have heard of my Father I have made known unto you."* [4]

In John 14 Jesus comforted the disciples about His soon departure from this world and spoke of the coming of *another* Comforter:

> *"And I will pray the Father, and he shall give you another Comforter, that he may abide with you for ever."* [5] *"He is the Holy Spirit, who leads into all truth. The world cannot receive him, because it isn't looking for him and doesn't recognize him. But you know him, because he lives with you now and later will be in you."* [6]

How could Jesus say that they already knew the Holy Ghost and "he lives with you now"?[7] Because Jesus was filled with the Holy Ghost;[8] therefore, the Holy Ghost was with the disciples whenever Jesus was with them.

The Holy Ghost would be *in* them, not just *with* them, as Jesus had been. He would be inside of them—not only comforting them in their sadness because Jesus had left them but also reminding them of what Jesus had said and telling them secrets gleaned from Jesus' relationship with His Father.

---

[4] John 15:15 KJV.
[5] John 14:16 KJV.
[6] John 14:17 NLT.
[7] John 14:17 NLT.
[8] See Luke 4:14.

JESUS IS YOUR FRIEND; HOLY GHOST IS YOUR FRIEND

When Jesus said the Father would send *"another Comforter"* He was saying, in effect, "After I am gone, you will have Holy Ghost in My place. He is another Comforter just like Me. He will never leave you."

This Friend would empower them to be like Jesus

> *"For God knew his people in advance, and he chose them to become like his Son."*[9]

This Friend would teach them everything about Jesus

> *"But when the Father sends the Advocate as my representative—that is, the Holy Spirit—he will teach you everything and will remind you of everything I have told you."*[10]

This Friend would give them Christ-like character qualities

Holy Ghost would develop in them character qualities of Jesus like fruit of the Spirit—love, joy, peace, patience, kindness, goodness, faithfulness, gentleness and self-control.[11]

This Friend would give them spiritual power like Jesus

Holy Ghost would impart to them the same spiritual gifts that they had seen operating in Jesus throughout his ministry—such as healing, the working of miracles, and discerning of spirits.[12]

---

[9] Romans 8:29 NLT.
[10] John 14:26 NLT.
[11] See Galatians 5:22-23.
[12] See 1 Corinthians 12.

3

I want you to put this together with me:

When Jesus said, *"But when the Comforter is come, whom I will send unto you from the Father"*[13] He was explaining the Holy Ghost in the context of Friendship.

First Jesus said, *"I have called you friends,"*[14] then He said, *". . . the Comforter . . . whom I will send unto you from the Father."*[15]

When the Holy Ghost comes, He does not represent Himself. He represents Jesus, our Friend. Therefore, Holy Ghost is my Friend.

This revelation of Friendship was not only for the disciples. It is for us, because after we are born again we have the potential to do whatever Jesus did by the power of the Holy Ghost working inside of us as our Friend.

> ***Jesus is present and dwells within you***
> ***through the Holy Ghost***
> ***whenever you are born again.***
> ***Holy Ghost has the same relevance to you***
> ***that Jesus has. He is just as real.***
> ***He is just as much of a Friend as Jesus.***
> ***He is God, just as Jesus is God,***
> ***but He has a different assignment.***

WHAT KIND OF FRIENDSHIP IS HOLY GHOST FRIENDSHIP?

You have relational value with the Father, Son, and Holy Ghost when you have given your life to Jesus. All of the authority and power of God is within your reach.

---

[13] John 15:26 KJV.
[14] John 15:15 KJV.
[15] John 15:26 KJV.

Instead of being a distant theological entity, God is your Friend, your Companion, and your Comforter.

Esteem and affection

When Holy Ghost is your Friend, you are connected to Him by affection and sentiments of esteem, respect and affection that lead you to desire His company as He desires yours. You seek to please Him and He brings you into the prosperity and spiritual power of God's Kingdom.

FRIEND—WEBSTER'S 1828 DICTIONARY

"One who is attached to another by affection; one who entertains for another sentiments of esteem, respect and affection, which lead him to desire his company, and to seek to promote his happiness and prosperity."[16]

"A friend loveth at all times. Prov. 17."

Love. Holy Ghost, your Friend, loves you at all times.

Truth. He is the "Spirit of Truth."[17] He is the Spirit of reality Who comes to you from the Father.

New life. When you have the Spirit of Truth as your Friend, you have a passion for the life of Jesus to become fully manifest in your life. Jesus doesn't come to be a part of your life. He comes to take over! Colossians 3:4 says, *"Christ, who is our life."* Jesus comes to be your whole life.

---

[16] *Webster's 1828 Dictionary*, s.v. "friend." Online at http://www.webster1828.com/websters1828/definition.aspx?word=Friend. Accessed September 2011.
[17] John 16:13 KJV.

FOCUS ON FRIENDSHIP

We need to refocus on cultivating a relationship with Holy Ghost to become our Best Friend.

YOUR INSIDER FRIEND

In the Old Testament, the Holy Spirit was usually active in the lives of prophets and patriarchs externally—in supernatural events like provision and success in battle.

In the New Testament, Jesus was outside of His disciples as the Son of Man.

However, after Pentecost, when you become a born-again believer in Jesus Christ, your Friend Holy Ghost comes inside. He gets so close to you that from then on He dwells with you forever. That is an extreme level of Friendship provided by Almighty God Himself.

Holy Ghost invites you to be an insider with God.

Sometimes Jesus preached to the masses, but at other times He would call just the Three to be with him—Peter, James, and John—such as on the Mount of Transfiguration[18] and in Gethsemane.[19] Jesus didn't take all of the disciples with Him everywhere, all the time, but now in this time of the Father's promise Jesus says the Holy Spirit, the Insider, is your Friend who will be with you all the time, forever.

---

[18] See Matthew 17.
[19] See Matthew 26.

A Friend you respect and reverence as holy

When Holy Ghost is your Friend, this is not a casual Friendship. Even though Jesus has opened the door for Him to be your Friend, you respect, honor, and reverence Him as God. God is holy. As you walk with Him on the Highway of Holiness, you become more holy, just as He is holy. Your relationship is characterized by holiness.

> *". . . and it shall be called the Highway of Holiness. The unclean shall not pass over it."*[20]

If you happened to be a friend of the President of the United States before he was elected, protocol would say that after he was elected you would call him "Mr. President," not use his first name.

When Jesus told the disciples that they were now His friends, at the same time He was still their Savior and Lord. They respected Him. They honored Him in their conversation. They obeyed His commands. They yielded to His Lordship over them. Later when John, *"the disciple whom Jesus loved,"*[21] was on the Isle of Patmos, he saw a vision of His Friend Jesus and was so overtaken with awe that he said, *"I fell at his feet as dead."*[22] John recognized his beloved Jesus but saw Him in manifestation as God in all His glory.

HOLY GHOST BAPTISM—PROMISE OF THE FATHER

The number one priority and command that Jesus left with His disciples—I mean the most important thing He wanted them to do first— was to "wait for the promise of the Father"[23] that He had told them about before.

---

[20] Isaiah 35:8 NKJV.
[21] John 21:20 KJV.
[22] Revelation 1: 17 KJV.
[23] Acts 1:4 KJV.

This promise of the Father was the Baptism in the Holy Ghost.

When the disciples met with Jesus before He ascended to Heaven, they asked Him if it was time for the earthly kingdom to be restored to Israel. However, He told them instead about greater power on a worldwide scale that they were about to receive when the Holy Ghost came upon them in a spiritual baptism.

> *"But ye shall receive power, after that the Holy Ghost is come upon you: and ye shall be witnesses unto me both in Jerusalem, and in all Judaea, and in Samaria, and unto the uttermost part of the earth."[24]*

That is a provision worthy of the God of the entire universe!

Holy Ghost is an eternal and unlimited Being

Holy Ghost has existed throughout all eternity. He has always been present on the earth since its Creation and all throughout Old Testament history until now.

Friendship with the Eternal God

Many Christians know that Holy Ghost has power. They know He provides gifts of the Spirit and fruit of the Spirit. They would be able to say that Holy Ghost does the Father's will just as Jesus did the Father's will.

However, this whole idea of the Holy Ghost as your Friend is another matter! This is about the cultivation of an airtight relationship! Even if you have read what Jesus said in John 14 and 15 about the Comforter, you have probably not

---

[24] Acts 1:8 KJV.

considered the implications that you are now a Friend of the great Holy Ghost Who created the world.

ONE GOD—FATHER, SON, AND HOLY GHOST— CREATED THE WORLD

"Hear, O Israel: The LORD our God is one LORD."[25]

God the Father at Creation. "In the beginning God created the heavens and the earth" (Genesis 1:1 KJV).

God the Son at Creation. "In the beginning was the Word, and the Word was with God, and the Word was God. The same was in the beginning with God. All things were made by him; and without him was not any thing made that was made. In him was life; and the life was the light of men" (John 1:1-4 KJV).

God the Holy Ghost at Creation. "And the earth was without form, and void; and darkness was upon the face of the deep. And the Spirit of God moved upon the face of the waters" (Genesis 1:2 KJV).

Man Made in the Image of God at Creation. "And God said, Let us *[plural]* make man in our image" (Genesis 1:26 KJV).

GOD'S RESTORATION OF A FRIENDSHIP BEFORE THE FALL

God—Father, Son, and Holy Ghost—made man in His image to be His Friend, but man sinned[26] and fell away from God and lost the opportunity for that great Friendship offer.

However, the Father's heart for the man and woman He created was still so full of love that He laid out a plan of redemption to restore that Friendship through the sacrifice of His Son Jesus for our sins.

---

[25] Deuteronomy 6:4 KJV.
[26] See Genesis 3.

"For God so loved the world, that he gave his only begotten Son, that whosoever believeth in him should not perish, but have everlasting life."[27]

Jesus became mankind's gateway of access to a restored Friendship with the Father. Jesus opened the door back to Friendship by His death on the cross.

"For since our friendship with God was restored by the death of his Son while we were still his enemies, we will certainly be saved through the life of his Son. So now we can rejoice in our wonderful new relationship with God because our Lord Jesus Christ has made us friends of God."[28]

That is why the temple curtain to the Holy of Holies split in half supernaturally from top to bottom when Jesus died. Access to God had been restored!

"Then Jesus shouted out again, and he released his spirit. At that moment the curtain in the sanctuary of the Temple was torn in two, from top to bottom."[29]

RELATIONSHIP BETWEEN FATHER, SON, AND HOLY GHOST

- The Father sent Jesus to be our Savior from sin.
- Jesus asked the Father to send the Holy Ghost to those who are saved through Him.
- When Holy Ghost comes, you receive power to carry out the wishes of God the Father and become like Jesus and His miraculous ministry on earth.

---

[27] John 3:16 KJV.
[28] Romans 5:10-11 NLT.
[29] Matthew 27:50-51 NLT.

THE TRIUNE, PERSONAL NATURE OF GOD

". . . God is a personal, infinite, eternal, self-existent, unchangeable, indivisible, omnipotent, omniscient, omnipresent, spiritual being Who is the creator and sustainer of the universe."[30]

". . . this one God exists eternally in three distinct Persons (Father, Son, and Holy Spirit), each of whom shares equally in all the divine attributes."[31]

Coalition on Revival
"Essentials of a Christian World View"

- Holy Ghost is the power force in the earth to carry out the wishes of God the Father.
- Holy Ghost is the vehicle Who takes you to the Father and makes that relationship real.
- Jesus made the way for Holy Ghost to accomplish what the Father wants done on earth.
- Now that Jesus has returned to Heaven, Holy Ghost follows up with you and disciples you *in the place of Jesus* back into God's image and likeness.

- The Father sets up everything.
- Jesus administrates everything.
- The Holy Ghost manifests everything.

---

[30] Article 4, "The Essentials of a Christian World View" (Coalition on Revival, P.O. Box 1139, Murphys, California 95247). Online at http://65.175.91.69/Reformation_net/default.htm. Accessed November 2011.
[31] Article 6, "The Essentials of a Christian World View" (Coalition on Revival, P.O. Box 1139, Murphys, California 95247). Online at http://65.175.91.69/Reformation_net/default.htm. Accessed November 2011.

ALWAYS REMEMBER TO RESPECT GOD AS INDEFINABLE

When my wife first met me, she was 15 and I was 16. She can tell you I was a wordsmith, meaning I loved to read the dictionary. I loved words and their definitions. I would try to blow her mind with big words that she didn't understand.

However, when I started getting into Scripture, I realized that only a few times did Jesus use a word of more than four syllables.

God imparts revelation through "knowing"

Revelation is not based on having a great vocabulary. It comes through knowing a great God.

Revelation is not cunning terminology. It comes when the Holy Ghost unveils something to you that agrees with Scripture and your spiritual understanding takes a leap into reality. Maybe you can explain it to somebody or maybe you can't, but you have a knowing inside.

True revelation is simply a knowing. There is not always articulation. You just know something is reality. Words have boundaries but God is limitless. He says He has no beginning and no ending. He says, *"I am the beginning and the end,"*[32] so words are a limitation.

God is love

When you are with someone you love, you don't always have to talk to communicate. A sense of love and familiarity fill the room when you are together, even if you don't define that love in words. That is what our Friendship with God is like.

---

[32] See Revelation 21:6.

God told Moses simply, "I AM"—You Can't Define Me

When Moses asked God what he should say to people who asked him the name of the God Who sent him, God replied, "I AM." In other words, God said, "You couldn't find a term for Me that could satisfy Me in any language. You couldn't find words that could explain Me well enough. Therefore, just tell them 'I AM.'"

> *"But Moses protested, 'If I go to the people of Israel and tell them, "The God of your ancestors has sent me to you," they will ask me, "What is his name?" Then what should I tell them?'*
> *"God replied to Moses, 'I AM WHO I AM. Say this to the people of Israel: I AM has sent me to you.'"* [33]

God is NOW!

The entire Godhead is forever *now*! Faith is now! Love is now! Hope is now! Holy Spirit is now! And my Friend is the Resource Person for the entire existence of God.

When you have a relationship with God, you are dealing with Somebody who creates language—words and definitions—but He is indefinable. The only way you can know Him is if He reveals Himself. That's why after Jesus reveals Himself to you as your Savior and He introduces Holy Ghost to you as your Friend, no mocking or contrary words or even the threat of death can make you deny that you are born again. You have experienced reality.

One person has said that a man with an experience is never at the mercy of a man with an idea!

---

[33] Exodus 3:13-14 NLT.

God is real even if you can't convince some skeptics

Some Christians bound by a religious mindset might challenge your salvation experience to see if it matches criteria they have learned from their denomination or their personal prejudices. They ask you, "Did you remember to do this? Did you do that? Did you apply the blood? Did you say I'm sorry? Did you repent of your sins? Did you let Him in as Savior and Lord?"

Other Christians don't believe you if you say you have been baptized in the Holy Ghost with the manifestations of speaking in tongues and prophecy. They don't believe in miracles or divine healing as you have ever since you received the Baptism in the Holy Ghost. They say, "That was for the First Century but it is not for today."

Even if people try to confuse you or try to make you conform to their understanding of how someone is born again or baptized in the Holy Ghost, when you have met Jesus in a real way and the Holy Ghost is your Friend, you can respond respectfully, "Listen, I'm saved. The Word confirms that the Person I met is Jesus. I have experienced the power of the Holy Ghost. I just obeyed the Father and received what He had promised."

THE FATHER'S PROMISE OF HOLY GHOST BAPTISM

When Jesus told His disciples to wait in Jerusalem until they were baptized with the Holy Ghost, this was a new level for them beyond repentance and receiving Jesus as Savior from sin.

Jesus saw the Baptism in the Holy Ghost as so important that before He ascended to the Father He *commanded* them to wait for it. He told them that it was something that God the Father Himself had promised to give them. *They must not miss this.*

"And, being assembled together with them, [Jesus] commanded them that they should not depart from Jerusalem, but wait for the promise of the Father, which, saith he, ye have heard of me. For John truly baptized with water; but ye shall be baptized with the Holy Ghost not many days hence."[34]

Prophecy of John about Jesus and Holy Ghost Baptism

John the Baptist prophesied about this Baptism in the Holy Ghost when he declared that while he baptized in water for repentance Jesus would baptize in the Holy Ghost and fire.[35] John said this powerful connection to God was coming:

"I indeed baptize you with water unto repentance: but he that cometh after me is mightier than I, whose shoes I am not worthy to bear: he shall baptize you with the Holy Ghost, and with fire."[36]

Thirsty for God, then filled with the flow of the Spirit

Jesus said our passion to be connected to God and to be filled with His Spirit are like the thirst for water. If you are spiritually thirsty enough, you will go after Jesus to get living water and He will baptize you in the Holy Ghost.

Jesus told the Samaritan woman at the well:

"Whosoever drinketh of this water shall thirst again: But whosoever drinketh of the water that I shall give him shall never thirst; but the water that I shall give him shall be in him a well of water springing up into everlasting life."[37]

---

[34] Acts 1:4-5 KJV.
[35] See Matthew 3:11.
[36] Matthew 3:11 KJV.
[37] John 4:13-14 KJV.

Jesus satisfies your thirst and you are baptized in the Holy Ghost. Then the Spirit can flow from you like a river, providing water for others who are thirsty for God.

> *"In the last day, that great day of the feast, Jesus stood and cried, saying, If any man thirst, let him come unto me, and drink. He that believeth on me, as the scripture hath said, out of his belly shall flow rivers of living water. (But this spake he of the Spirit, which they that believe on him should receive: for the Holy Ghost was not yet given; because that Jesus was not yet glorified.)* "[38]

Progression from believing in Jesus to Holy Ghost Baptism

First, leading up to Jesus' command to wait in Jerusalem until they were baptized in the Holy Ghost, even before He went to the cross, Jesus told His disciples that He was going away but He would send the Holy Ghost.

Then, after His resurrection, Jesus breathed on His disciples and said, "Receive ye the Holy Ghost."[39] Before He ascended He commanded them to be baptized in the Holy Ghost before they launched into ministry.

Then Holy Ghost came at Pentecost and was with them in power throughout their journeys in the book of Acts.

Here is the progression:

- Receive Jesus as your Savior and Lord.
- Be baptized in the Holy Ghost and receive power.
- Develop your Friendship with the Holy Ghost so that you can become like Jesus and fulfill the will of God for your ministry in earth as it is in Heaven.

---

[38] John 7:37-38 KJV.
[39] John 20:22 KJV.

SUPERNATURAL EXPERIENCES IN THE BOOK OF ACTS

Beginning at Pentecost, several incidents occurred in the early Church where people were baptized in the Holy Ghost with speaking in tongues.

Pentecost

Jesus had commanded the disciples to wait in Jerusalem for the promise of the Father, so they assembled in an upper room and waited together for several days. Finally, on the day of Pentecost, they were baptized with the Holy Ghost and fire. Pentecost is the Greek name for the Jewish Festival of First Fruits or Festival of Weeks[40] that comes seven weeks or 50 days after Passover,[41] when Jesus was crucified. Fifty is the number for the Jubilee—the Lord's release.[42]

> *"And when the day of Pentecost was fully come, they were all with one accord in one place. And suddenly there came a sound from heaven as of a rushing mighty wind, and it filled all the house where they were sitting. And there appeared unto them cloven tongues like as of fire, and it sat upon each of them. And they were all filled with the Holy Ghost, and began to speak with other tongues, as the Spirit gave them utterance."[43]*

The Lord released or Jubileed the disciples into ministry on the 50th day by baptizing them in the Holy Ghost.

Paul's ministry to Ephesus

Paul was not present in the upper room at Pentecost.

---

[40] See Exodus 34:22 and Deuteronomy 16:10.
[41] Jesus said to His disciples, "As you know, Passover begins in two days, and the Son of Man will be handed over to be crucified" (Matthew 26:2 NLT).
[42] See Deuteronomy 15:2.
[43] Acts 2:1-4 KJV.

He was converted later in another supernatural experience when the same Holy Ghost came and filled Him.

Later, as an apostle, Paul went to Ephesus where he found people who had experienced John's baptism of repentance but were not yet baptized in the name of Jesus and had not heard about the Holy Ghost. He baptized them in Jesus' name and when he laid hands on them they began to speak with other tongues and prophesy.

> *"He said unto them, Have ye received the Holy Ghost since ye believed? And they said unto him, We have not so much as heard whether there be any Holy Ghost. And he said unto them, Unto what then were ye baptized? And they said, Unto John's baptism.*
>
> *"Then said Paul, John verily baptized with the baptism of repentance, saying unto the people, that they should believe on him which should come after him, that is, on Christ Jesus.*
>
> *"When they heard this, they were baptized in the name of the Lord Jesus. And when Paul had laid his hands upon them, the Holy Ghost came on them; and they spake with tongues, and prophesied."[44]*

SUPERNATURAL SENSITIVITY TO HOLY GHOST

Those were clearly supernatural encounters with God when the Holy Ghost came upon people and they began to speak with tongues.

Paul described the gifts of the Holy Ghost in detail in 1 Corinthians 12 and 14. Here is one quote:

> *"But the manifestation of the Spirit is given to every man to profit withal. For to one is given by the Spirit the word of wisdom; to another the word of knowledge by the same Spirit; To another faith by the same Spirit;*

---

[44] Acts 19:1-6 KJV.

18

*to another the gifts of healing by the same Spirit; To
another the working of miracles; to another prophecy;
to another discerning of spirits; to another divers kinds
of tongues; to another the interpretation of tongues.* "[45]

Holy Ghost Baptism takes you past your human limitations

There are two levels of life. First there is natural life
and then there is spiritual life. The Bible says that we usually
receive knowledge first at the level of the natural human mind.
Afterwards, with the help of our Friend, we can receive
knowledge from the supernatural realm of the Spirit.

*"Howbeit that was not first which is spiritual, but that
which is natural; and afterward that which is
spiritual."* [46]

When Holy Ghost comes, you are forced to consider
the spiritual realm beyond what you see in the natural realm—
what is visible to your natural mind as a descendant of Adam
after the Fall. Where you were once predominantly earthly, like
the fallen Adam, in Christ you can become a heavenly person.

*"Adam, the first man, was made from the dust of the
earth, while Christ, the second man, came from
heaven. Earthly people are like the earthly man, and
heavenly people are like the heavenly man. Just as we
are now like the earthly man, we will someday be like
the heavenly man."* [47]

The Bible says that *"we will someday be like the
heavenly man."* By the power of the Holy Ghost, you are being
transformed into a heavenly man like Jesus. You are being
changed from a predominantly natural person to a
predominantly spiritual person who thinks and acts like Jesus.

---

[45] 1 Corinthians 12:7-10 KJV.
[46] 1 Corinthians 15: 46 KJV.
[47] 1 Corinthians 15:46-49 NLT.

Holy Ghost Baptism awakens your supernatural sensitivity

Some scholars and theologians approach the Bible like an earthly man. They have an analytical perspective. They appreciate its soundness and historical accuracy but never see with spiritual eyes what the Father has promised through the Holy Ghost Baptism. I am not trying to force-feed those people who limit themselves to what the Bible says on the surface, but I have something to offer those with the humility to see what I am saying in terms of a greater spiritual reality.

An advantage of humility—an open mind to the Spirit

I quoted at the beginning of this book from Isaiah 57 that God chooses to dwell with the humble:

"I live in the high and holy place with those whose spirits are contrite and humble.
I restore the crushed spirit of the humble and revive the courage of
those with repentant hearts."[48]

Those who are the most humble and broken are often the most sensitive to spiritual reality. They can receive with simple faith what Jesus said. That is why the 20th century revival of Pentecost with the experience of the Baptism in the Holy Ghost and speaking in tongues was led by a humble Black American, William Seymour, at Azusa Street in Los Angeles, beginning in 1906.

The spiritual concept of Holy Ghost as your Friend may not be something that you can see at first by intellectual competence but I hope you will eventually accept this, because it is reality. I am not risking eternity for temporary gain to try to convince somebody of a concept that doesn't agree with Scripture or doesn't take you into the face of Jesus.

---

[48] Isaiah 57:15 NLT.

If you have a heart for Jesus and a passion for what Jesus reveals, I believe you will see that this is the truth.

Jesus talked about Holy Ghost in terms that described His humility. Holy Ghost is God with all that power yet He sees His purpose as glorifying Jesus. Jesus said about Him:

> *"He shall glorify me: for he shall receive of mine, and shall show it unto you. All things that the Father hath are mine: therefore said I, that he shall take of mine, and shall show it unto you."*[49]

Don't you want to be in a place of receptivity when Holy Ghost comes to show you the real Jesus?

Holy Ghost is real to those who suffer and keep believing

Holy Ghost will help you to make the Bible and Jesus a reality to you. You may have the right information. You may even have the right interpretation. But if it doesn't lead you to the Person of Christ and help you to grow in the character of Christ, something inside of you is still unsettled. You may have become settled to the degree that you can win an argument over another Christian but not to the degree that you can see Jesus more clearly and see other people through His eyes.

I grew up among humble people who were not well educated but they understood the Bible better than some theologians. God gave them supernatural ability because they were baptized in the Holy Ghost and passionate about knowing God. They had simple, childlike faith that the Bible was true and they never wavered from that belief. That is how they were able to survive when their lives were filled with so much hardship. They knew God was with them.

---

[49] John 16:14-15 KJV. Spelling updated.

WHERE HOLY GHOST FRIENDSHIP BEGINS

I remember years ago opening a thick book on the Kingdom of God and reading the grandiloquent words and complex terminology. On the surface it looked as if that author really knew something, but after reading just a page or two, I saw that he didn't have a relationship with the Person he was talking about. That doesn't mean that he was saying something that wasn't true or even that he wasn't biblical. However, the true essence of the Person of the Holy Spirit was missing from his writing. His book had some information but it didn't draw me closer to God. I could have studied it and become intellectually astute. I could have become mentally more informed. I could have gained superior understanding, but I would not have drawn closer to the Holy Ghost as my Friend.

Some educated people enjoy logic. They like rhetoric. They could probably create a PowerPoint teaching about my Friend and say, "Here are seven things I want to show you about the Holy Ghost." However, one of their greatest challenges would be to stop relying so much on their mind and their natural information that they miss the heart and Friendship of the Holy Ghost. They need to become what they are writing and talking about, like Haggai:

> *"Then spake Haggai the LORD'S messenger in the LORD'S message unto the people . . ."[50]*

In effect, Haggai was saying, "I am not just saying a message. I am the message that I am saying."

The Baptism is only a gateway to Holy Ghost Friendship

The Baptism of the Holy Ghost is a gateway to your relationship with my Friend, but it is not the relationship itself.

---

[50] Haggai 1:13 KJV.

Any Friendship takes time to develop. You are introduced to Holy Ghost Friendship with the Baptism in the Holy Ghost but that is only the beginning. You have a lifetime ahead of you to become closer Friends. In fact, this is one Friendship that extends into eternity. You are Friends forever.

You build your Friendship by common interests. You desire the same things He desires. You cry out with passion, "Why aren't there more miracles? Why aren't more people saved? Why don't we have a spiritual awakening? What must I do so you can use me to bring revival?"

Fear of the supernatural blocks entry to this Friendship

If you are a more conservative Christian, you may not want to make that much noise. You probably don't want to do anything undignified or beyond the level of your mental understanding. You may be reluctant to venture into the realm of the supernatural.

What you call your faith in Christ might be based only on the letter of the Word. You may have made a conscious decision to receive Jesus as Savior but in reality you feel as if you are placing your confidence in something that is still dark to you. Even though Jesus said it and you believe it, maybe you are not so sure of it.

Fear and spiritual ignorance cause people to ignore Holy Ghost or to keep Him at a distance at the level of doctrine or a footnote. Even those who have tremendous mental understanding of the Bible often don't seem to know the Person of Christ or have a Friendship with Holy Ghost because they have not released control to Him. They don't understand what an adventure they are missing!

GOD'S GOT BLESSINGS FOR YOU

Holy Ghost is the manager of the resources of Heaven. He doesn't just have money. He is the Money Magnate. If you need healing, He is the Healer. If you need lands, He owns all the property of the earth.

Holy Ghost is the blessing of Abraham

He is the blessing of Abraham!

"That the blessing of Abraham might come on the Gentiles through Jesus Christ; that we might receive the promise of the Spirit through faith."[51]

He is the blessing and He has the blessings. Once you receive Him you are tied into the handler of the resources of Heaven. Your Friendship with Him puts you at the highest level in every category. He not only knows who you are. He is developing you into the person you should become through faith and providing the resources you need to do God's work.

Responsibilities and assignments of the Godhead

Remember, all members of the Godhead have different responsibilities and assignments.

- God the Father—Operations
- God the Son—Administration
- God the Holy Ghost—Manifestation

"And there are differences of administrations, but the same Lord. And there are diversities of operations, but it is the same God which worketh all in all. But the manifestation of the Spirit is given to every man to profit withal."[52]

---

[51] Galatians 3:14 KJV.
[52] 1 Corinthians 12:5-7 KJV.

However, you can't keep them in any one category. They are all-in-one Big Picture Thinkers.

- While you are looking at your situation, God the Father sees the operations at work in the whole scenario.
- When you are off base, Jesus is thinking about administration.
- When you want to know why something is not happening, you need to go the Holy Ghost.

Holy Ghost teaches you and reminds you about Jesus

"But when the Father sends the Advocate as my representative—that is, the Holy Spirit—he will teach you everything and will remind you of everything I have told you."[53]

Holy Ghost has come to help you to know Jesus. He sets you free to know Jesus. The Advocate confirms to you that Jesus is God. He speaks on behalf of Jesus. He affirms Jesus' integrity, His power, and His love! When you have confidence that you have a relationship with Jesus, you can thank my Friend, Holy Ghost!

Your Advocate stands up for you like a lawyer

Jesus said in John 15:

"But I will send you the Advocate [or Comforter or Encourager or Counselor]—*the Spirit of truth. He will come to you from the Father and will testify all about me."[54]*

---

[53] John 14:26 NLT.
[54] John 15:26 NLT. Includes footnote in brackets.

"Advocate" is a translation of the Greek word
Paracletos that is used for Holy Ghost. You might place a
different connotation on the word "Advocate" as compared to
"Comforter," but when somebody stands up for you in court,
doesn't that give you comfort? Isn't that what friends do? They
stand up for you. In other words, your Advocate is your Divine
Defense Attorney.

> *As the old mothers used to say,*
> *"We have an Attorney standing up for us*
> *Who has never lost a case!"*

When the devil accuses you, Holy Ghost fights with truth

In every case where Jesus was challenged with
accusations, people had the same witness and testimony as
Pilate, "I find no fault in this man."[55]

Jesus never did anything wrong. That is your potential
with Holy Ghost as your Friend. They will find no fault in you.
Holy Ghost works in you to develop your holiness and also
convinces you that you are never alone when facing
adversaries.

> *"And when they bring you unto the synagogues, and*
> *unto magistrates, and powers, take ye no thought how*
> *or what thing ye shall answer, or what ye shall say:*
> *For the Holy Ghost shall teach you in the same hour*
> *what ye ought to say."[56]*

As you come to know Jesus and take on the ways of
your Friend, you never feel alone when someone falsely
accuses you. When you are on the side of Truth, you are on the
same side as Jesus.

When someone accuses you of wrongdoing, those
accusations will always be false. If a court tries to bring

---

[55] Luke 23:4 KJV.
[56] Luke 12:11-12 KJV.

charges against you, you will have the same testimony as Jesus—they found no fault in me. They have no legitimate case. If they win, it is an injustice because you were innocent in every way.

Holy Ghost comes to live in you and make you His temple

When Holy Ghost is your Friend, your body has to cease putting fleshly demands on you like the lust of the flesh, the lust of the eyes, and the pride of life.[57] You are the temple of God now.

> *"Don't you realize that your body is the temple of the Holy Spirit, who lives in you and was given to you by God? You do not belong to yourself, for God bought you with a high price. So you must honor God with your body."*[58]

He purifies your character

God can get so much more out of your life than He is able to do presently. With the Holy Ghost as our Friend, I believe that God is going to raise up sons and daughters who really know Him—not just know *about* Him, but who seek after Him, pray, and study the Word to see what is right and then do it. They will allow the Holy Ghost to cleanse them from sin. They will allow Him to speak through them in prophecies and words of life.

Then they will be able to clearly call out truth to this generation as Holy Ghost sees it.

.

---

[57] See 1 John 2:16.
[58] 1 Corinthians 6:19-20 NLT.

WHAT THIS MEANS TO YOU

What is the will of God for your life? God wants to accomplish more in your life than making you happy, healing your emotional wounds, paying your bills, and giving you a nice husband or wife.

While that may be a part of the restoration process after you are saved, that was not Jesus' focus. You are saved to become like Jesus and finish His work.

Saved and baptized in the Holy Ghost to become like Jesus

"For whom he did foreknow, he also did predestinate to be conformed to the image of his Son, that he might be the firstborn among many brethren."[59]

God's greater purpose for your life is to use you to reach people for Him, get them saved by preaching the Gospel of salvation in Jesus Christ, and then disciple them as they are empowered by the Holy Ghost into the Christian life.

***You cannot successfully disciple someone
until he is saved and baptized in the
Holy Ghost and has entered into
Holy Ghost Friendship.***

Manifesting the *gifts* of the Spirit

Everyone needs a deeper, more powerful relationship with God beyond just being saved. That is why Jesus commanded the disciples to wait until they were baptized in the Holy Ghost. They needed that power to fulfill the Great Commission and reach the world.

When you receive the Baptism in the Holy Ghost, you enter a new level of service. You can receive gifts of the Spirit:

---

[59] Romans 8:29 KJV.

- Word of wisdom
- Word of knowledge
- Faith
- Healing
- Working of miracles
- Prophecy
- Discerning of spirits
- Speaking in unknown tongues
- Interpretation of tongues[60]

In this book I am not attempting to explain all of the manifestations of the gifts of the Holy Spirit. I just want to make you aware of them. (See also Chapter 11.)

Manifesting the *fruit* of the Spirit

Holy Ghost bears fruit in your life that grows out of your relationship with Him. *This fruit is for others.* In Galatians 5, Paul used words like **love** (you love others, not just receive love), **joy** (from doing the will of God), **peace** (with God), **patience** (with spouse, children, friends, etc.), **kindness** (to those in need), **goodness** (to others, just like Jesus), **faithfulness** (you can be trusted), **gentleness** (in dealings with others), and **self-control** (you don't lose your temper, you don't give up on people or on God). (See also Chapter 13.)

> *"But the Holy Spirit produces this kind of fruit in our lives: love, joy, peace, patience, kindness, goodness, faithfulness, gentleness, and self-control. There is no law against these things!*
> *"Those who belong to Christ Jesus have nailed the passions and desires of their sinful nature to his cross and crucified them there. Since we are living by the Spirit, let us follow the Spirit's leading in every part of our lives."[61]*

---

[60] See 1 Corinthians 12:7-10.
[61] Galatians 5:22-25 NLT.

ETERNAL WORLD OF HOLY GHOST IS THE REAL WORLD

Friendship with Holy Ghost is not the same as human friendship. He is not even mystical about it. He is equipping you to live in the real world with that fruit. His world is the only reality!

Living in the "real world" is living in the realm of eternity

My Friend Holy Ghost is the Spirit of truth, the Spirit of "the real world," which is the eternal world, not the earth. When your Friend Holy Ghost makes your darkness light, your faith is no longer mysterious. Your faith becomes as real to you as pinching yourself.

I have heard so many Christians say, "I hear what you say about this faith stuff but I have to live in the real world." Maybe you have said that yourself. You think it is one thing to go to church on Sunday but on Monday you have to work "in the real world" and the next day you have to pay your bills. You don't want to hear it when somebody says, "But my God shall supply all your need according to his riches in glory by Christ Jesus."[62] You reply, "I know all that and I have been saying that, too, but I still have to pay my bills."

What you are saying in effect is that money in your hands is your real world. To that degree, you have not made the Holy Ghost your Friend and asked Him to take you into the true eternal realm of reality. To that degree, your faith is still intellectualism or emotion. It is mental acquiescence.

Holy Ghost is always there with you and in you

Holy Ghost is a Friend you always want around. You reveal to Him your secret heart. You always do whatever He says so you can show Him your allegiance. You never want Him to leave. When God says, "I will never leave thee, nor

---

[62] Philippians 4:19 KJV.

forsake thee"[63] you respond fervently, *"Yes! God will never leave me or forsake me!"*

When you respond to His offer with a confession like that, it shows Him that you are in agreement with Him. You recognize that He has done something for you and you want what He is offering.

Isn't that true about any friend? No friend wants a one-sided relationship. He wants to know that you like him around.

A Friend Who has your back

Maybe you have friends whom you hate to see coming because they always stay too long. You want to tell them, "I'm tired of you being around all the time. Go to your own place. Don't you have a home?"

However, a real friend doesn't affect you that way. You say, "Man, I like this person being around me. I mean, this is someone I trust. This is someone I can talk to about anything. This is someone I know who has my back." Even ghetto people understand that!

Most people don't know Holy Ghost at that level of Friendship, but they can. You can know Him because Jesus made a way for God to be in you as your Friend.

> *"There shall not any man be able to stand before thee all the days of thy life: as I was with Moses, so I will be with thee: I will not fail thee, nor forsake thee."[64]*

A Friend Who gives you access to the mind of Christ

Some Christians love to say, "I serve the Lord Jesus," but they may not see Jesus as their Best Friend Who shares their life with them. Jesus redefined discipleship in His relationship with His disciples.

---

[63] Hebrews 13:5 KJV.
[64] Joshua 1:5 KJV.

Jesus said to His disciples: *"I call you not servants; for the servant knoweth not what his lord doeth."*[65]

They had been like servants. Hardly anyone allows a servant to have the same level of access as a friend. You don't want a servant prying into all your private business. If someone cleans your house you don't tell her the same things you tell your best friend. That's not the kind of relationship you have with a servant.

A Friend Who tells you the Father's thoughts

Some dictionary definitions of "friend" could take you off track. They include terms like associate, sidekick, lover, and other terminology. Jesus defined friendship for us. He said, "I call you friends" and then He explained what He meant. A servant doesn't know what his Master is doing all the time and doesn't know what the Master knows, but a best friend of the Master knows. That is how He defined our Friendship with Him and what benefits He would give us as His friends.

"Henceforth I call you not servants; for the servant knoweth not what his lord doeth: but I have called you friends; for all things that I have heard of my Father I have made known unto you."[66]

Jesus said, *"I have called you friends: for all things that I have heard of my Father I have made known unto you."* Think back to all those things Jesus might have heard from His Father. Those are things that your Friend the Holy Spirit is going to make known to you when He reveals the mind of Christ to you. What an awesome privilege!

"'Who can know the LORD'S thoughts? Who knows enough to teach him?' But we understand these things, for we have the mind of Christ."[67]

---

[65] John 15:15 KJV.
[66] John 15:15 KJV.
[67] 1 Corinthians 2:16 NLT.

A Friend Who lights your way ahead

There is too much obscurity in the body of Christ for people who are supposed to have direct access to God as Holy Ghost friends. Let me be personal. In my own life there is still too much that I don't know about the internal, invisible world. There's still too much darkness there for me. I want more light on where the angels are now, what they are doing, and how many of them are with me right now. I want to understand the Bible at a deeper level. I need more light to see the road ahead.

"The way of the righteous is like the first gleam of dawn, which shines ever brighter until the full light of day. But the way of the wicked is like total darkness. They have no idea what they are stumbling over."[68]

A Friend Who helps you remember what is important

Jesus said the Holy Ghost will "bring all things to your remembrance, whatsoever I have said unto you."[69] Some people have a great memory for Scripture and it gives them light to live by. In your case you don't need a great memory. You just need a great Friend. You can memorize Scripture and we do teach kids to do that, but you can't remember it all. Your solution to imperfect Scripture memorization is be a friend of the One who remembers it all. He says He will bring all things to your remembrance. That's His job and it's your job to have Him as your Best Friend.

A Friend Who gives you power to do good deeds

God anointed Jesus with the Holy Ghost and with power. When you get to know the Holy Ghost, He brings His

---

[68] Proverbs 4:18-19 NLT.
[69] John 14:26 KJV.

33

power with Him into your relationship and anoints you for power and good deeds.

> *"How God anointed Jesus of Nazareth with the Holy Ghost and with power: who went about doing good, and healing all that were oppressed of the devil; for God was with him."*[70]

If we are honest about it, the Church today doesn't seem to be demonstrating that level of power that Jesus had in His life. Since we have the same Holy Ghost it would be legitimate to ask our Friend, "Why isn't the power working with us the same way it worked with Jesus?" We can express a concern like that to God as a legitimate request. We are not accusing Him but we are saying to Him that we need the power that we know He wants to give us.

A Friend Who gives you power over demonic oppression

Again, the Bible says, *"How God anointed Jesus of Nazareth with the Holy Ghost and with power: who went about doing good, and healing all that were oppressed of the devil; for God was with him."*[71] When Holy Ghost is our Friend, we have the same assignment as Jesus—to go about doing good and healing all who are oppressed of the devil!

Clearly, Holy Ghost anointed Jesus to deal with all demonic oppression. Can Holy Ghost anoint me to deal with demonic oppression if I am under His leadership? Yes. That may seem like an extravagant request in a day when the Church spends so little time dealing with the demonic realm, but it is needed. All you have to do is consider current news events to see how the devil is driving people to do evil.

---

[70] Acts 10:38 KJV.
[71] Acts 10:38 KJV.

A Friend Who gives you passion for a global awakening

I believe that as we accept and practice this revelation of my Friend, Holy Ghost, we will celebrate Him and promote His work of making Jesus known. Our improved relationship with Holy Ghost will give us an even greater passion for a global awakening.

We need to find a new way to go after Holy Ghost power in the Church so that we can reach the world with the message of Jesus.

If my Friend Jesus cannot be with me, yet He left me a provision for the power I need to follow in His steps, it is not wrong for me to ask my Friend for that power today!

If your Friend Holy Ghost is taking you on an assignment, He knows your weaknesses. He will help you to overcome them and administrate your assignment by providing you with His power. Paul admitted to the church at Corinth:

> *"I came to you in weakness—timid and trembling. And my message and my preaching were very plain. Rather than using clever and persuasive speeches, I relied only on the power of the Holy Spirit. I did this so you would trust not in human wisdom but in the power of God."[72]*

Paul didn't pretend he was perfect and he didn't focus on building a following. He focused on driving people to God because God would always be there for them.

Holy Ghost is not going to take you somewhere, leave you by yourself, and then let you get beat up by the devil and the darkness that Jesus came to destroy. He understands you and He knows what you need to overcome the devil and bring yourself and others into the abundant life.

---

[72] 1 Corinthians 2:3-5 NLT.

"The thief cometh not, but for to steal, and to kill, and to destroy: I am come that they might have life, and that they might have it more abundantly."[73]

---

[73] John 10:10 KJV.

2

MY FRIEND IS GOD MOST HOLY AND A HUMBLE PERSON, NOT A THING

*"There are 'friends' who destroy each other,
but a real friend sticks closer than a brother."*[1]

*"For I am the LORD your God.
You must consecrate yourselves and
be holy, because I am holy."*[2]

Holy Ghost "shall not speak of himself."[3]

When Jesus introduced His disciples to this Friend, Holy Ghost, He used personal pronouns. "*He* will guide you." "*He* will tell you." "*He* will bring Me glory." Holy Ghost is a Person of the Godhead but He is not trying to show off or be known. He is humble like Jesus:

*"Who being in the form of God, thought it not robbery
to be equal with God: But made himself of no
reputation."*[4]

---

[1] Proverbs 18:24 NLT.
[2] Leviticus 11:44 NLT.
[3] John 16:13 KJV.
[4] Philippians 2:6-7 KJV.

Holy Ghost will let somebody use Him in a great way and allow that person to get all the credit for what Holy Ghost did. He will never bang His chest and say like a rookie basketball player getting a great shot, *"That was me who did that!"* You will have to find Him to discover what He did.

> *". . . he shall not speak of himself; but whatsoever he shall hear,* that *shall he speak: and he will show you things to come. He shall glorify me: for he shall receive of mine, and shall show* it *unto you."*[5]

Holy Ghost seeks no reputation but promotes Jesus

In Philippians 2, Paul talks about how Jesus made Himself of no reputation. Holy Ghost also stays in the background, not trying to be seen, not wanting to get credit. He is doing all of His work for Jesus. He is doing it to promote Jesus. He is coming in the place of Jesus. He is fully Jesus but at the same time He is fully Holy Spirit. That is powerful!

People who want recognition are empty. When Jesus made Himself of no reputation, He knew that the key to carrying the Father's power and the Father's authority was to lose His desire for wanting to be Somebody. Jesus wants you to understand that you can handle power only when you don't want it. You can be somebody in God when you make yourself nobody.

Hardly any pastor or Christian leader today in the fivefold ministry of apostle, prophet, pastor, teacher, or evangelist has it as a goal to make himself of no reputation. The main idea in our culture is to make yourself known. In the personal estimation of most people, they have failed if they don't become well known or don't become famous as an expert in their field. Humility is a formula for failure in their minds, but in the economy of God it is a formula for success.

When Holy Ghost comes, Jesus said, He is a Person characterized by absolute humility.

---

[5] John 16:13-14 KJV. Contemporary spelling.

*"When the Spirit of truth comes . . . He will not speak
on his own but will tell you what he has heard. He will
tell you about the future. He will bring me glory by
telling you whatever he receives from me. All that
belongs to the Father is mine; this is why I said, 'The
Spirit will tell you whatever he receives from me.'"*[6]

A Christian who is always talking about himself is to
that extent not like Jesus and not Spirit-led. If you are a real
Christian, recognition by man is not important to you. All you
want is the secret approval of God.

CHARACTERISTICS OF EVERY GOOD FRIENDSHIP

One way to understand Holy Ghost Friendship is to
look at a few of the characteristics of any good friendship.
These include qualities of love and companionship, willingness
to be corrected, comfort, and trust.

Love and companionship. My wife is my best friend
other than Holy Ghost. I like to play golf so she encourages me
to play and sometimes she comes along and rides in my golf
cart. In our friendship, she likes to be with me whether she
plays golf or not. She also likes to travel with me when I go to
speaking engagements. She does not have to do anything. She
just wants to be with me.

Willingness to be corrected. Friends want the truth
about their faults. They are never closed. That is the kind of
close relationship that Holy Ghost wants with us.

Comfort. Holy Ghost is reliable, available, and
consistent. He fulfills all of the expectations that Jesus had
when He left Him in charge as the Comforter in His place.

---

[6] John 16:13-15 NLT.

Trust. Jesus said that Holy Ghost would tell us secret things from His conversations with His Father. Any friend needs to know that he can trust you with his secrets.

12 BENEFITS OF HOLY GHOST FRIENDSHIP

1. As you listen to your Friend, you learn about Jesus and begin to remember things that Jesus said and did.

2. As you spend time with Him, you become more like Him, which also means you become more like Jesus.

3. You learn what Jesus and His Father talked about in secret.

4. You become more inwardly holy.

"HOLY"—STRONG'S GREEK #40 *HAGIOS*

"Hagios; holy, set apart, sanctified, consecrated. It has a common root, *hag-*, with *hagnos* (53), chaste, pure.
Its fundamental ideas are separation, consecration, devotion to God, and sharing in God's purity and abstaining from earth's defilement. Contrast to *hieros* (2413), *hagiois* has moral significance while *hieros* has only ritual significance." [7]

Stephen, "full of the Holy Ghost" [8]

---

5. You develop a lifestyle characterized by holiness.

6. Your faith increases.

---

[7] *Hebrew-Greek Key Word Study Bible, King James Version,* Spiros Zodhiates, ed. (Chattanooga, TN: AMG Publishers, 1991), s.v. "40 *hagios.*"
[8] Acts 7:55 KJV.

7. You operate in the gifts of the Holy Spirit.

8. You begin to do good deeds as a natural expression of your faith—not because you are following rules or laws that tell you to do good deeds but because you want to do them out of your heart.

"For the Scriptures say, 'It is through faith that a righteous person has life.' This way of faith is very different from the way of law, which says, 'It is through obeying the law that a person has life.'"[9]

9. You are able to love others abundantly out of a pure heart. You learn how to be a good friend to others because you have the greatest Friend of all in your life.

"And the Lord make you to increase and abound in love one toward another, and toward all men, even as we do toward you."[10]

10. You become a trustworthy person of integrity.

11. You understand why God created you and perceive what kind of destiny He has planned for you.

12. You live with a sense of eternity that gives you a godly framework for your personal and professional life.

12 STEPS TO A HOLY GHOST FRIENDSHIP

Here are some steps you can take to build a great Friendship with my Friend, Holy Ghost.

1. Get introduced to Him by being born again.

---

[9] Galatians 3:11-12 NLT.
[10] 1 Thessalonians 3:12 KJV.

2. Have the supernatural experience of being baptized in the Holy Ghost.
3. Get the sin out of your life.
4. Pay attention to Him because you can't have a Friend Whom you ignore. Give Him more attention than anyone else on the earth.
5. Cultivate your Holy Ghost Friendship by spending time with Him daily.
6. Talk to Him often because He is always there and He is a great listener. When you talk to your Friend, you get to know Him better.
7. Don't talk all the time. Also listen. Cultivate silence to hear His voice. (If you don't listen, that shows you don't believe He is there.)

". . . study to be quiet."[11]

8. Be sensitive to Him and do what He says.
9. Develop a trust relationship through interaction. He sees He can trust you as you develop a track record with Him. He told you to do something and you did it.
10. Learn His tendencies because you are a real friend.
11. Honor Him as the Third Person of the Godhead.
12. Be careful not to offend Him because blasphemy against the Holy Ghost is never forgiven.[12]

12 HOLY GHOST CHARACTER QUALITIES

My Friend has all of the character qualities necessary for building the best Friendship.

1. Humility

Jesus said, *". . . for he shall not speak of himself."*[13]

---

[11] 1 Thessalonians 4:11 KJV.
[12] See Matthew 12:31.
[13] John 16:13 KJV.

2. Sensitivity to others' needs and a commitment to pray

   "And the Holy Spirit helps us in our weakness. For example, we don't know what God wants us to pray for. But the Holy Spirit prays for us with groanings that cannot be expressed in words."[14]

3. Love, joy, peace, patience, kindness, goodness, gentleness, faithfulness, self-control (fruit)[15]

   "For the fruit of the Spirit is in all goodness and righteousness and truth."[16]

4. Filling our hearts with love

   "For we know how dearly God loves us, because he has given us the Holy Spirit to fill our hearts with his love."[17]

5. Giving comfort

   The Comforter (*Parakletos* in Greek) means One called alongside to help. Holy Spirit is the believer's indwelling Paraclete to help us. You are comforted because He is on your side fighting for you.

   Jesus said, *"It is expedient for you that I go away: for if I go not away, the Comforter will not come unto you; but if I depart, I will send him unto you."[18]*

6. Helping people—including the poor—and sticking with them forever

---

[14] Romans 8:26 NLT.
[15] See Galatians 5:22-23.
[16] Ephesians 5:9 KJV.
[17] Romans 5:5 NLT.
[18] John 16:7 KJV.

Jesus said, *"I will ask the Father, and He will give you another Helper, that He may be with you forever."*[19]

7. Power-source for believers

   Jesus said, *"And now I will send the Holy Spirit, just as my Father promised. But stay here in the city until the Holy Spirit comes and fills you with power from heaven."*[20]

8. Provider of spiritual gifts[21]

   "But one and the same Spirit works all these things, distributing to each one individually just as He wills."[22]

9. Communicator who speaks your language

   At Pentecost, *"When they heard this sound, a crowd came together in bewilderment, because each one heard them speaking in his own language."*[23]

10. Advocate standing up for you before your adversaries, regardless of the cost

11. Eternal Spirit[24]

    ". . . that he may abide with you forever."[25]

12. Holy and imparter of holiness

    "And that ye may put difference between holy and unholy, and between unclean and clean."[26]

---

[19] John 14:16 NASB.
[20] Luke 24:49 NLT.
[21] See 1 Corinthians 12-14 and other chapters in the Bible and this book.
[22] 1 Corinthians 12:11 NASB.
[23] Acts 2:6 KJV.
[24] See Hebrews 9:14.
[25] John 14:16 KJV. Spelling updated.

HOLY GHOST HELPS YOU BECOME HOLY TO PLEASE GOD

Holiness is not the same as "law-based" accountability to authorities or accountability partners. Although you can use those systems to help you develop, it is your *personal* calling to be holy. A more contemporary word you might understand is integrity. Christ-like, internal holiness comes through cultivating a relationship with your Friend Holy Ghost.

> ". . . but like the Holy One who called you, be holy yourselves also in all your behavior."[27]

Your response to God's call to holiness is yielding

If you want to know God's truth and you want Him to use you, yield your heart and mind inwardly to Him. Know Him in that secret closet where you surrender all of yourself to Him. Know Him in sacrificial prayer and dedication.

The Christian walk cannot be mastered and God cannot be understood solely with an effort of the will and the analysis of the mind. You cannot possibly discern everything God wants with human logic. He defies logic, even though He is logical. To know God, you have to discern Him inwardly, through yielding your heart to the working of the Holy Ghost.

There is something incredibly beautiful about people who are yielded to the will and purposes of God through the workings of our Friend, Holy Ghost. Hardships no longer have power to destroy them. Trials no longer take them out of the character of Christ-likeness. A heavenly glow of peace shows up on their faces that could not have come from any of the world's cosmetics!

> "Thy people shall be willing in the day of thy power, in the beauties of holiness from the womb of the morning: thou hast the dew of thy youth."[28]

---

[26] Leviticus 10:10 KJV.
[27] 1 Peter 1:15 NASB.
[28] Psalms 110:3 KJV.

Reigning with God requires holiness

The Bible says that someday we will rule and reign with Jesus, but first we have to be changed into His holiness.

"God reigneth over the heathen: God sitteth upon the throne of his holiness."[29]

"But ye are a chosen generation, a royal priesthood, an holy nation, a peculiar people; that ye should show forth the praises of him who hath called you out of darkness into his marvelous light."[30]

In 2011 a royal wedding took place in London when Prince William and Catherine were married. The media made it public knowledge that their premarital relationship was not characterized by holiness. That is not what God expects of those who are in His royal family through the Holy Ghost.

Every Christian has to die to sin before he can live in newness of life just as Jesus had to die before He could be resurrected. Holy Ghost doesn't raise anything that is not dead.

Paul said that even as Christ died for him, when he came to Christ he had to die, also.

The first place that every Christian must come to after he is born again is Galatians 2:20—"I am crucified with Christ."

"Sanctify yourselves therefore, and be ye holy: for I am the LORD your God."[31]

---

[29] Psalms 47:8 KJV.
[30] 1 Peter 2:9 KJV. Spelling updated.
[31] Leviticus 20:7 KJV.

Holy ground is the place where godly people must live!

"And the captain of the LORD's host said unto Joshua, Loose thy shoe from off thy foot; for the place whereon thou standest is holy. And Joshua did so."[32]

Holiness and deliverance are linked

"But upon mount Zion shall be deliverance, and there shall be holiness; and the house of Jacob shall possess their possessions."[33]

The Spirit of holiness raised Jesus from the dead

"And declared to be the Son of God with power, according to the spirit of holiness, by the resurrection from the dead."[34]

Overflowing love toward others leads to a holy heart

"And may the Lord make your love for one another and for all people grow and overflow, just as our love for you overflows. May he, as a result, make your hearts strong, blameless, and holy as you stand before God our Father when our Lord Jesus comes again with all his holy people."[35]

Holiness in leaders pleases God

God is calling His Church to a new obedience that relates to holiness. I can see how God has protected me over

---

[32] Joshua 5:15 KJV.
[33] Obadiah 17 KJV.
[34] Romans 1:4 KJV.
[35] 1 Thessalonians 3:12-13 KJV.

the years, not only in keeping me holy but also in keeping me from relationships with ministers who have fallen into sin.

Looking back, I can see how He helped me beginning at the time when I was saved as a young man. At that time I went to ministers I knew and excitedly talked about Jesus and told them what had happened to me. However, instead of being excited with me they put me down. One said, "You will be all right. You will calm down after a while." He could not identify with anything I said. Later that same minister became a homosexual and a drug dealer. He and another man were found dead in a river near his house with cinderblocks tied to them.

Here was a man ostensibly called by God to be a great preacher and great singer for the Lord. Was his death caused by God? God didn't have to deal with him. I didn't have to respond to him. The Bible says that eventually the soul that sins will surely die.[36] When a minister compromises the Gospel and becomes an unrighteous scoffer of the life of Christ, eventually the judgment of God will come upon him—if not in this world then in the next.

> *"For the time is come that judgment must begin at the house of God: and if it first begin at us, what shall the end be of them that obey not the gospel of God?"[37]*

I made the decision that if nobody else would stand with me, if nobody else would be right according to the way I saw it in the Scriptures, I would still stand for Jesus.

> *"But keep on the alert at all times, praying that you may have strength to escape all these things that are about to take place, and to stand before the Son of Man."[38]*

> *"Her priests have violated my law, and have profaned mine holy things: they have put no difference between the holy and profane, neither have they shewed*

---

[36] See Ezekiel 18:20.
[37] 1 Peter 4:17 KJV.
[38] Luke 21:36 NASB.

difference *between the unclean and the clean, and have
hid their eyes from my sabbaths, and I am profaned
among them.* "[39]

Your holiness affects others

Someone else's destiny relates to your obedience.
Saul was the people's choice but he proved to be
disobedient to God and unholy. David was God's choice.

> *"And the LORD said unto Samuel, How long wilt thou
> mourn for Saul, seeing I have rejected him from
> reigning over Israel? Fill thine horn with oil, and go, I
> will send thee to Jesse the Bethlehemite: for I have
> provided me a king among his sons."* [40]

Samuel went out and found David whom God had
chosen as the next king. God had sent Samuel out with oil so
that he could consecrate David into office.

> In the Old Testament, every time you
> stepped into an office you had to be
> consecrated. Leaders today want the
> office without the consecration.

Today we have men with big bellies calling themselves
prophets but they are undisciplined over the plate and over
food. They don't know what fasting is. They don't know how
to separate themselves from people to seek God only. They
don't go in the fulness of the Holy Ghost into the wilderness to
fight the devil so they don't emerge in the power of the Holy
Ghost. They have counterfeit power.

---

[39] Ezekiel 22:26 KJV.
[40] 1 Samuel 16:1 KJV.

"Preserve my soul; for I am holy: O thou my God, save thy servant that trusteth in thee."[41]

"They stumble because they do not obey God's word, and so they meet the fate that was planned for them.
"But you are not like that, for you are a chosen people. You are royal priests, a holy nation, God's very own possession. As a result, you can show others the goodness of God, for he called you out of the darkness into his wonderful light."[42]

Holiness gives you access to God's secrets

You please God when you give up your rights to please your flesh and make an absolute commitment to deal with your rebellion and unbelief so that you can be holy.

Most people don't even know what that means. When you have meekness and attentiveness in prayer, God can trust you and Holy Ghost can teach you and give you the secrets that the Father spoke to Jesus.

THIS FRIENDSHIP REQUIRES THE FEAR OF GOD

God knows that there is a correlation between the purity of your life and your fear of God, your respect for God.

In order to know God, you need to be free from sin.

In order not to sin, you need to fear God. You need the reality of God—the awesome God who created the world and everything in it, including you.

"Who else has held the oceans in his hand?
Who has measured off the heavens with his fingers?

---

[41] Psalms 86:2 KJV.
[42] 1 Peter 2:8-9 NLT.

Who else knows the weight of the earth
or has weighed the mountains and hills on a
scale?
Who is able to advise the Spirit of the Lord?
Who knows enough to give him advice or teach
him?
Has the Lord ever needed anyone's advice?
Does he need instruction about what is good? . . .
"'To whom will you compare me?
Who is my equal?' asks the Holy One.
"Look up into the heavens.
Who created all the stars?
He brings them out like an army, one after another,
calling each by its name.
Because of his great power and incomparable strength,
not a single one is missing. . . .
"Have you never heard?
Have you never understood?
The Lord is the everlasting God,
the Creator of all the earth.
He never grows weak or weary.
No one can measure the depths of his
understanding."[43]

I am afraid of Somebody Who can say, "Let there be light" and there is light. I am afraid of Somebody Who held the oceans in His hand or Who knows the weight of the earth and has spread out the heavens like a curtain.

The fear of God drives you to renounce sin

To the extent that sin is not a reality to you, you will not fear God and will not be able to develop this Friendship. Cleanse yourself from sin and you will find that Holy Ghost is your real Friend.

---

[43] Isaiah 40:12-14, 25-26, 28 NLT.

"Having therefore these promises, dearly beloved, let us cleanse ourselves from all filthiness of the flesh and spirit, perfecting holiness in the fear of God."[44]

As God makes Himself known to you, you cannot help but fear Him. You have a mature respect for God like an adult who respects his father and would never knowingly disappoint him. You want to live righteously before God and you want to please Him because He is your Holy Friend.

Sin against the Holy Ghost has eternal consequences

In the early Church, a married couple named Ananias and Sapphira sold some property and tried to fool the apostles into believing that they were donating all the proceeds. However, Peter was in a Friendship with Holy Ghost so the Spirit of Truth revealed what had happened.

"But Peter said, Ananias, why hath Satan filled thine heart to <u>lie to the Holy Ghost</u>, and to keep back part of the price of the land? Whiles it remained, was it not thine own? and after it was sold, was it not in thine own power? why hast thou conceived this thing in thine heart? thou hast not lied unto men, but unto God. And Ananias hearing these words fell down, and gave up the ghost: and great fear came on all them that heard these things. And the young men arose, wound him up, and carried him out, and buried him."[45]

Blasphemy against the Holy Ghost is an unforgivable sin

When people are not afraid of God, the reality of God is far from them. Woe to any Christian who doesn't walk with

---

[44] 2 Corinthians 7:1 KJV.
[45] Acts 5:3-6 KJV. Emphasis added.

a sense of purity and holiness. God must not be real to you. Holy Ghost is not your Friend. He is not guiding you.

Jesus requires respect for Holy Ghost. Jesus said:

> *"Wherefore I say unto you, All manner of sin and blasphemy shall be forgiven unto men: but the blasphemy against the Holy Ghost shall not be forgiven unto men.*
> *"And whosoever speaketh a word against the Son of man, it shall be forgiven him: but whosoever speaketh* against *the Holy Ghost, it shall not be forgiven him, neither in this world, neither in the world to come."*[46]

HOW THIS RELATES TO YOU

Maybe you look around at the news and the worldwide persecution of Christians and you see a need for revival. What should you do personally to prepare for God to use you?

Make yourself ready for revival by abandoning yourself to the preparations, which includes seeking God for His holiness so that you can access His power.

> *"But ye shall receive power, after that the Holy Ghost is come upon you: and ye shall be witnesses unto me both in Jerusalem, and in all Judaea, and in Samaria, and unto the uttermost part of the earth."*[47]

Every ordinance of God comes in the closet of isolation. Your calling from God has to come from your personal time with God in total dedication and devotion.

If a prophetic word doesn't bring you to a new dedication, that word has missed its mark. Even if you fall on

---

[46] Matthew 12:31-32 KJV.
[47] Acts 1:8 KJV.

the floor "under the power" then you fell under the power of the devil and when you got up you were the same devil as you were before you fell.

When you become more consecrated, you increase your ability to hear God's voice. Jesus could hear God because He was consecrated. He is holy, harmless, and undefiled.[48] He teaches you how to be like Him through the ministry of your Friend, Holy Ghost.

When you become like Jesus, you become more holy, more harmless, and more undefiled, and you can hear God more clearly as an inevitable result of the process of consecration. What steps will you take today to be like Him?

"But as many as received him, to them gave he power to become the sons of God, even to them that believe on his name: Which were born, not of blood, nor of the will of the flesh, nor of the will of man, but of God."[49]

---

[48] See Hebrews 7:26.
[49] John 1:12-13 KJV.

3

MY FRIEND AT THE
CREATION OF THE WORLD

"For the LORD *is God, and he created the heavens
and earth and put everything in place."[1]*

My Friend Holy Ghost was present at the creation of the heavens and the earth. All Three Persons of the Godhead were there—Father, Son, and Holy Ghost.

God the Father. *"In the beginning God created
the heavens and the earth."[2]*

God the Son. *"In the beginning was the Word,
and the Word was with God, and the Word was
God. The same was in the beginning with God.
All things were made by him; and without him
was not any thing made that was made."[3]*

God the Holy Ghost. *"And the earth was
without form, and void; and darkness was
upon the face of the deep. And the Spirit of
God moved upon the face of the waters."[4]*

---

[1] Isaiah 45:18 NLT.
[2] Genesis 1:1 NLT.
[3] John 1:1-3 KJV.
[4] Genesis 1:2 KJV.

Three phases of creation

Here are three key phases of creation related to Holy Ghost Friendship:

1. God's creation of the earth.
2. God's creation of male and female in His image.
3. God's re-creation of sinners through Jesus Christ by the Holy Ghost.

CLIMAX OF CREATION—MAN IN THE IMAGE OF GOD

The Bible says that God made the world to be lived in. God created all of creation and then topped it off by saying, "Let us make man in our image, after our likeness. Nothing else in the world will be defined like him." God built all of creation on the expectation that man would live there and God and man would be in fellowship as friends because mankind was made in His image.

First God created everything that man would ever need for time and eternity. Then He made the man. In effect, He made the man without need. Man would never have to live on the asking side. He could always be on the producing side. He would have a leader's supply-side mentality. His conversations with the Holy Ghost would be leadership conversations about fulfilling the will of God.

Authority of first man from His relationship with God

When you build your relationship with God through Friendship with the Holy Ghost, you can return to the authority God gave Adam before the Fall. Your conversations with God can change the focus from your personal needs as a sinner to consideration of national affairs and global concerns. This is in line with the dominion that God gave the first man and woman over the whole earth.

"So God created man in his own image, in the image of God created he him; male and female created he them. And God blessed them, and God said unto them, Be fruitful, and multiply, and replenish the earth, and subdue it: and have dominion over the fish of the sea, and over the fowl of the air, and over every living thing that moveth upon the earth."[5]

Progression from man's creation to man's jurisdiction

- First, God created everything that man would need.
- Next, God made man.
- Then God set man's jurisdictional realm of dominion over every living thing moving.

God not only said let us make man excellent, good-looking, as "cut" as a body-builder and smart as an Einstein.

He said, "Let us make man like Us! Because if he is like Us, then he can do what We can do."

God went further than that. He said to man, "Here is your jurisdictional responsibility. You are to take dominion over everything that creeps upon the Earth, everything that's in the sea, everything that's above the Earth."

Significance of being made in God's image

Genesis 1:26 captures the concept of the Trinity ("Let *us* make man in *our* image") and also emphasizes that man is made in the image of God ("in our image, after our likeness").

---

[5] Genesis 1:28-29 KJV.

"And God said, Let us <u>make</u> man in our image, after our likeness. . . ."[6]

MAKE
(Hebrew Word *Asah*)

Strong's Concordance, Old Testament Hebrew number 6213 **asah,** *aw-saw'*; a prim. root; to do or make, in the broadest sense and widest application (as follows):—accomplish, advance, appoint, apt, be at, become, bear, bestow, bring forth, bruise, be busy, X certainly, have the charge of, commit, deal (with), deck, + displease, do, (ready) dress (-ed), (put in) execute(-ion), exercise, fashion, +feast, [fight-]ing man, +finish, fit, fly, follow, fulfil, furnish, gather, get, go about, govern, grant, great, + hinder, hold ([a feast]), X indeed, + be industrious, + journey, keep, labour, maintain, make, be meet, observe, be occupied, offer, + officer, pare, bring (come) to pass, perform, practice, prepare, procure, provide, put, requite, X sacrifice, serve, set, shew, X sin, spend, X surely, take, X throughly, trim, X very, + vex, be [war-]ior, work(-man), yield, use.

". . . and let them have dominion over the fish of the sea, and over the fowl of the air, and over the cattle, and over all the earth, and over every creeping thing that creepeth upon the earth. So God created man in his own image, in the image of God created he him; male and female created he them."[7]

---

[6] Genesis 1:26 KJV. Emphasis added.
[7] Genesis 1:26-27 KJV.

Startling Implications of Made "In His Image"

Because man is made in the image of God,
he can dominate over everything else on earth.

Because man is made in the image of God,
he can know the Father, Son, and Holy Ghost.

Because man is made in the image of God,
he can have Friendship with the Holy Ghost.

Notice the emphasis on God's nature in us by the repetition of these phrases:

- "in our image"
- "after our likeness"
- "in his own image"
- "in the image of God"

This emphasis from Genesis is crucial to understanding that you have the capacity for a real Friendship with Holy Ghost and the goal of that Friendship is to be like God.

God created male and female in His image, blessed them, and gave them an assignment to have children:

THE LIFE MANDATE

"And God blessed them, and God said unto them, Be fruitful, and multiply, and replenish the earth, and subdue it: and have dominion over the fish of the sea, and over the fowl of the air, and over every living thing that moveth upon the earth."[8]

---

[8] Genesis 1:28 KJV.

The first priority in creation is fruitfulness. Let's be specific. While we can talk about the built-in standard of fruitfulness as character, the outcome standard of fruitfulness is having children. God made Adam to be like Him. Every other child would be Adam's fruit and be like him.

A child comes from God to parents from the union of the marriage bed. Pregnancy is fruitfulness. Every new child who is conceived is a blessing ordained by God.

> *"And God blessed them, and God said unto them, Be fruitful, and multiply."*[9]

"Fill the earth with Adamic children," God was saying! He gave Adam a blessing and a mandate for new life. If you don't agree with the *Life Mandate* you are an enemy of creative order and the Godhead! Holy Ghost is the Life-giver in the earth. He has to fight against you if you oppose life because God is the Author of Life. God ordains it, Jesus authorizes it, Holy Ghost does it!

The redemptive story confirms the Life Mandate

Jesus says, *"I am come that they might have life, and that they might have it more abundantly."*[10]

Jesus' healing, deliverance, and restoration ministry is all about fulfilling the Life Mandate.

The abortion or killing of babies in the womb is a work of Satan who comes to bring death to the world as an enemy of the cause of God and God's people. Every abortionist is a murderer in the Kingdom of God and therefore Holy Spirit has to fight against him or destroy him!

In the United States, Black Americans have proportionately killed more of their own babies in the womb than any other race of people. They have lost the value of life. They don't know why they should live! Sure, they should stop

---

[9] Genesis 1:28 KJV.
[10] John 10:10 KJV.

60

having sex outside of marriage like every other race. But every other race doesn't destroy their babies at the same rate.

In the last 30 years Black Americans have killed 15-20 million babies in the womb. It is a tragedy to a people group with so much potential.

> *"But where sin abounded, grace did much more abound."[11]*

I was conceived out of wedlock. I came the wrong way, but I am the right result. Millions have heard God's Word as a result of my mom letting me live.

> ***I say to Black America,***
> ***Let the babies live!***
> ***Let the babies live!***

Turn the deathstyle into a lifestyle in your people. Get on God's side in every area of life and fulfill your God-given destiny. You are a valid people group! You have a destiny. God will not fail you if you give your life totally to Him. Your call is global! Holy Ghost bids you come! It is your time! The devil is a liar. He will lose. God will win concerning you.

Blessings!

> *"Blessed be the God and Father of our Lord Jesus Christ, who hath blessed us with all spiritual blessings in heavenly places in Christ."[12]*

Ability to reproduce yourself is God-given

Reproduction applies to both natural and spiritual children. God said, "I'm not only going to make you like Me

---

[11] Romans 5:20 KJV.
[12] Ephesians 1:3 KJV.

and give you responsibility. I am also going to give you the ability to reproduce yourself, so that every human being who comes after you on the Earth will be the progeny of your seed.

"Whatever you are in your nature is what everyone born from your seed will be.

"Whatever Holy Ghost Friendship you enjoy with me, all of your descendants can enjoy with Me if they are born again."

LIFE IS GIVEN TO EVERY PERSON BY GOD

"And I believe in the Holy Ghost,
the Lord, and Giver of life."

THE NICENE CREED

The breath of life in Adam

After God made the first man from the dust of the earth, He breathed life into him and he became a living person.

"And the LORD God formed man of the dust of the ground, and breathed into his nostrils the breath of life; and man became a living soul."[13]

Adam was not originally a creature of the environment who required air to live. Before the Fall[14] man was a creature kept alive by the breath of God. Adam before the Fall was not defined by external limitations like air. He had received an eternal nature from the breath of God that kept him alive physically and spiritually.

---

[13] Genesis 2:7 KJV.
[14] See Genesis 2-3.

Spiritual cost of opposing life

Elihu said, *"For the Spirit of God has made me, and the breath of the Almighty gives me life."[15]*

God breathes life into a child before he is born. Before a baby is ever exposed to the air he is already alive inside his mother's womb. That is why abortion is a crime against the Holy Ghost.

Psalm 104 says God gives us breath

"When you give them your breath, life is created, and you renew the face of the earth."[16]

David wrote that God formed him in the womb

"You made all the delicate, inner parts of my body
and knit me together in my mother's womb.
Thank you for making me so wonderfully complex!
Your workmanship is marvelous—how well I
know it.
You watched me as I was being formed in utter
seclusion,
as I was woven together in the dark of the
womb.
You saw me before I was born.
Every day of my life was recorded in your
book.
Every moment was laid out
Before a single day had passed."[17]

---

[15] Job 33:4 NLT.
[16] Psalm 104:30 NLT.
[17] Psalm 139:13-16 NLT.

Jeremiah wrote that God set him apart before he was born

> *"The Lord gave me this message:*
>
>> *"'I knew you before I formed you in your mother's womb.*
>> *Before you were born I set you apart and appointed you as my prophet to the nations.'"*[18]

Holy Ghost breathes spiritual life into every Christian

> *"And when [Jesus] had said this, he breathed on* them, *and saith unto* them, *Receive ye the Holy Ghost."*[19]

You come alive in Christ when you are born again. You are a new person with a new life!

> *"At one time we thought of Christ merely from a human point of view. How differently we know him now! This means that anyone who belongs to Christ has become a new person. The old life is gone; a new life has begun!"*[20]

The coming of the Holy Ghost into believers is described as wind from God—something you can't explain.

> *"Jesus replied [to Nicodemus], 'I assure you, no one can enter the Kingdom of God without being born of water and the Spirit. Humans can reproduce only human life, but the Holy Spirit gives birth to spiritual life. So don't be surprised when I say, 'You must be born again.' The wind blows wherever it wants. Just as you can hear the wind but can't tell where it comes*

---

[18] Jeremiah 1:4-5 NLT.
[19] John 20:22 KJV.
[20] 2 Corinthians 5:16-17 NLT.

from or where it is going, so you can't explain how people are born of the Spirit. "[21]

ABORTION MAKES YOU AN ENEMY OF THE HOLY GHOST

In the public arena today two debates that are labeled political issues are actually issues that come under the jurisdiction of my Friend, Holy Ghost.

- The nature of marriage (a man and a woman)
- The life of the child in the womb

Marriage and an unborn child's right to live are not primarily political issues at all. They were determined by creative order. There is no debate about what God has declared.

Abortion is not a political issue; it is a creation issue

Pastors are not following the Holy Ghost when they push back from centuries of tradition regarding human life. They say, "I don't want to discuss abortion. It's a political issue." It is *not* a political issue. It is an issue of creative order.

I would ask them, "Are you saying that there are things more important than a baby being killed in the womb? You say you speak for God to your congregation, but God is the Author of life. He created that life and He is willing to take responsibility for that child. God allowed conception to come. You cannot take that life."

The baby in the womb is a unique human being who never existed before. He is made in the image of God. He has the DNA of that man and woman. The seed of the man and the egg of the woman have joined together and now cells in this new person are dividing and multiplying. A new life has begun.

---

[21] John 3:5-8 NLT.

This unborn child is a living entity, totally separate from his mother. Any preacher or other person, no matter what his title, who does not agree to let that baby come is an enemy of the Holy Ghost.

When you make Holy Ghost your enemy He fights you

Jesus said, *"I am come that they might have life, and that they might have it more abundantly."*[22]

There are two kinds of life—natural and spiritual. Holy Ghost is the Giver of both. If you kill that baby, you destroy something that He created. You have usurped the place of God. You have made the Holy Ghost your enemy and He is forced to fight against you.

Abortion is sin and requires repentance but can be forgiven

Align yourself on the side of Jesus. If you have destroyed life in the past, that was sin. Get that straight with Jesus within your own heart. Come into agreement with what I am saying because what I am saying is in the Bible. If there was a pregnancy, for whatever reason, God allowed a new life to be conceived. Whatever purpose He had in mind can never be fulfilled if you don't let that baby come.

God can choose to bring a baby the wrong way

Every child who is conceived has a right to come out. If a woman is raped and there is conception, that happened because God allowed it. God is the Author of life. He is willing to take responsibility for every child He creates. Even though the natural father did something wrong to that woman, God allowed conception to occur. Therefore, let that baby live!

---

[22] John 10:10 KJV.

Anyone who does not want to raise a child is dealing with other issues that they may need to resolve, but the issue of life is not in their hands. It is in God's hands.

Jesus has a prostitute in His family line—Rahab.

God told the prophet Hosea to marry a prostitute named Gomer and then God allowed conception. He said, "I want you to have another baby and let there be conception." He used it as a prophetic witness of something He wanted to say.

God defined marriage and has not changed His mind

You cannot find a single instance in the Bible where God condoned marriage between two people of the same gender. Everywhere a relationship between two people of the same sex is mentioned it is in a negative context. God defined marriage in Genesis and He has not changed His mind.

"Then the LORD God said, 'It is not good for the man to be alone. I will make a helper who is just right for him.' So the LORD God formed from the ground all the wild animals and all the birds of the sky. He brought them to the man to see what he would call them, and the man chose a name for each one. He gave names to all the livestock, all the birds of the sky, and all the wild animals. But still there was no helper just right for him.

"So the LORD God caused the man to fall into a deep sleep. While the man slept, the LORD God took out one of the man's ribs and closed up the opening. Then the LORD God made a woman from the rib, and he brought her to the man.

"'At last!' the man exclaimed.
"'This one is bone from my bone,
and flesh from my flesh!
She will be called "woman,"
because she was taken from 'man.'"

> *"This explains why a man leaves his father and mother and is joined to his wife, and the two are united into one."*[23]

God is the potter; you are His clay

God says clearly throughout the Bible, "I am the Creator. I have the power to do this. You cannot possibly see into the future to determine what God will do through this child's life. You can't even define your own lifetime unless I give you My understanding. You don't have a clue about your tomorrow, nor can you interpret your yesterday."

> *"Who are you, a mere human being, to argue with God? Should the thing that was created say to the one who created it, 'Why have you made me like this?'"*[24]

> *"What sorrow awaits those who try to hide their plans*
> *from the Lord, who do their evil deeds in the*
> *dark!*
> *"'The Lord can't see us,' they say.*
> *"'He doesn't know what's going on!'*
> *"How foolish can you be?*
> *"He is the Potter, and he is certainly greater*
> *than you, the clay!*
> *"Should the created thing say of the one who made it,*
> *"'He didn't make me'?*
> *"Does a jar ever say,*
> *"'The potter who made me is stupid'?"*[25]

---

[23] Genesis 2:18-24 NLT.
[24] Romans 9:20 NLT.
[25] Isaiah 29:15-16 NLT.

GET RIGHT NOW BEFORE YOU STAND BEFORE THE LORD

Whatever you believe now will have to be addressed in the Great Day. Your Friend is trying to lead you into an understanding that will get you right with God in that day when all people have to give recompense and stand before the Lord.[26]

Change the way you think until you think like God

You can't understand your Friend Holy Ghost unless you have been born again and your thinking has been changed to the eternal realm where God lives as a new creation. Nicodemus told Jesus he did not understand His language. He was a great scholar but he asked a foolish question about returning to his mother's womb. Jesus was not speaking about physical rebirth. He was talking about restoration to the Spirit's realm where man lives with an eternal mindset.

> *"Jesus replied, 'I tell you the truth, unless you are born again, you cannot see the Kingdom of God.'*
> *"'What do you mean?' exclaimed Nicodemus. 'How can an old man go back into his mother's womb and be born again?'*
> *"Jesus replied, 'I assure you, no one can enter the Kingdom of God without being born of water and the Spirit. Humans can reproduce only human life, but the Holy Spirit gives birth to spiritual life. So don't be surprised when I say, "You must be born again." The wind blows wherever it wants. Just as you can hear the wind but can't tell where it comes from or where it is going, so you can't explain how people are born of the Spirit.'"[27]*

---

[26] See Revelation 22:12.
[27] John 3:3-8 NLT.

He must be born again so that he could start over and his thinking could be like God. This is unexplainable to anyone like Nicodemus who is limited to an earthly mindset.

HOW THIS RELATES TO YOU

Align yourself with Jesus and His abundant life. Stay on the side of God. If you have participated in an abortion in the past, either yourself or someone you encouraged or assisted, it is not the unpardonable sin. Confess it and get straight with God and your own heart. Bring yourself into agreement with what God has said in the Bible and then move out in newness of life.

> *"The LORD brings death and makes alive;*
> *he brings down to the grave and raises up. . . .*
> *"For the foundations of the earth are the*
> *LORD'S; upon them he has set the world."*[28]

See yourself and your children not as cosmic accidents in evolution but chosen people whom God created for a purpose and a destiny. Every child who is conceived has a destiny from God. We have the opportunity to fulfill that destiny with the help of our Friend, Holy Ghost. You are a prophetic representation of the One Who created you, saved you, sustains you, and uses you to bring others into the Kingdom of God through new life in Christ.

Say to the Lord, "You saved me and You can use me to change a whole generation to bring glory to Your name."

---

[28] 1 Samuel 2:6, 8 NIV.

SECTION 2.
HOLY GHOST AND JESUS

4

MY FRIEND GAVE MARY
A SON—JESUS

"1. I believe in God the Father, Almighty,
Maker of heaven and earth:
2. And in Jesus Christ,
his only begotten Son, our Lord:
3. Who was conceived by the Holy Ghost,
born of the Virgin Mary."

THE APOSTLES CREED[1]

Holy Ghost was with Jesus at conception and throughout His time on earth. Although Mary was a virgin we know that she conceived the child Jesus in her womb by the Holy Ghost.

"And the angel answered and said unto her,
The Holy Ghost shall come upon thee, and the power
of the Highest shall overshadow thee: therefore also
that holy thing which shall be born of thee shall be
called the Son of God."[2]

---

[1] "The Apostles Creed." Online at http://www.ccel.org/creeds/apostles.creed.html. Accessed October 2011.
[2] Luke 1:35 KJV.

Before Mary became the mother of Jesus, God saw something different about her that caused Him to choose her out of all the women of the earth. He sent the angel Gabriel to speak to her about her destiny. Through the Holy Ghost, Mary became the carrier of the One who was going to meet the needs of the whole society for eternity. She found favor with God.

> *"'Don't be afraid, Mary,' the angel told her, 'for you have found favor with God!'"*[3]

She had the substance to carry in her womb the last Adam. What God made physically out of the dust of the ground in Genesis He made by the spoken word of the angel in the womb of this woman Mary.

The Immaculate Conception

The conception of Jesus is called the Immaculate Conception. No human sperm entered Mary's body by sexual intercourse. The words brought by Gabriel came from God into the womb of this woman's ears. In God's sight she was qualified to receive a God-said.

The word or the sperm or the seed of Jesus was conceived not only in her natural womb but also in her spirit. Jesus was both spiritual and natural because His conception came by words of spirit and life.

> *"'Don't be afraid, Mary,' the angel told her, 'for you have found favor with God! You will conceive and give birth to a son, and you will name him Jesus. He will be very great and will be called the Son of the Most High. The Lord God will give him the throne of his ancestor David. And he will reign over Israel forever; his Kingdom will never end!'*
>
> *"Mary asked the angel, 'But how can this happen? I am a virgin.'*

---

[3] Luke 1:30 NLT.

74

> *"The angel replied, 'The Holy Spirit will come upon you, and the power of the Most High will overshadow you. So the baby to be born will be holy, and he will be called the Son of God.'"*[4]

The word that came to Mary was a spirit word that related to the destiny of God inside her natural physical body. She was to carry Him physically so that He would be birthed forth naturally.

Nothing is impossible with God and a yielded vessel

Mary was called into a place of revelation where she had to receive something beyond her understanding that was coming through the Holy Ghost. However, the issue was not her mind. The issue was her heart. In God's eyes her heart was good ground to receive a God-said, a word from God.

Gabriel told Mary about the birth of John the Baptist:

> *"'What's more, your relative Elizabeth has become pregnant in her old age! People used to say she was barren, but she has conceived a son and is now in her sixth month. For nothing is impossible with God.'"*[5]

Mary responded:

> *"'I am the Lord's servant. May everything you have said about me come true.' And then the angel left her."*[6]

---

[4] Luke 1:30-35 NLT.
[5] Luke 1:36-37 NLT.
[6] Luke 1:38 NLT.

Holy Ghost brought this to pass

"And the angel departed from her."[7]

Why was the angel able to depart? His mission was accomplished. Mary had become good ground to become pregnant with the destiny of God in the womb of her belly.

The angel's words had changed how she saw herself and she received spiritual and natural seed into her, *"according to thy word."*[8]

She did not see herself in the same way. Now she saw herself as God saw her.

She had become good ground to become pregnant with the destiny of God in the womb of her belly.

She said, in effect, "According to thy word I no longer define myself. I see myself as Almighty God sees me. Now I understand who I am. The Holy Ghost has come upon me. It shall come to pass as God has said."

JESUS GREW UNDER THE INFLUENCE OF THE HOLY GHOST

As Jesus grew, Mary sowed into Him biblical foundations to allow Him to fulfill the will of God.

At age 12, Jesus went into the Temple in Jerusalem and talked intelligently to the learned men. He had a revelation of who He was and the authority God had given Him.

However, Jesus submitted Himself to His earthly parents when they found Him in the temple and told him it was time to leave. Jesus, the King of Glory, had to humble Himself and obey human parents, even though He knew more than they knew.

---

[7] Luke 1:38 KJV.
[8] Luke 1:38 KJV.

*"And all who heard Him were astonished at His
understanding and answers. So when they saw Him,
they were amazed; and His mother said to Him, 'Son,
why have You done this to us? Look, Your father and I
have sought You anxiously.' And He said to them,
'Why did you seek Me? Did you not know that I must
be about My Father's business?' But they did not
understand the statement which He spoke to them.
Then He went down with them and came to Nazareth,
and was subject to them, but His mother kept all these
things in her heart."*[9]

Jesus had the ability to know He was on an assignment
from God, even as a child, yet He never raised up against His
parents and the role that the Holy Ghost had given them to
fulfill in His life.

HOW THIS RELATES TO YOU

Something about this woman Mary's life relates to
you. If you see this as just a baby story, then you're totally
missing it. Right now, God sees you. You have been called to
bring into existence some purpose of God and you are the
physical, visible manifestation of an invisible intent from God.
You are to birth forth something by the Holy Ghost that is seen
and read of men. You are to bring it into reality so that the will
of God can be carried in the womb of your spirit until you
bring it to birth.

When the Holy Ghost comes upon you, you respond,
"Be it unto me according to thy word." Your heart agreement
to receive seed from the Holy Ghost will require that you move
beyond a survival mentality or being bound to gender, race,
economics, or circumstances. You will have to move to a place
where you can see yourself fulfilling the will of God.

---

[9] Luke 2:47-51 NKJV.

If you are born again but you
don't understand Friendship
with the Holy Ghost,
you will have eternal life, but you may never
find your place of purpose and significance.
Someone will always have to meet your needs
because you will always be thinking about
what you don't have, not realizing that
you know Someone personally Who has
the substance to fulfill the earth.

Mary was submitted to the sovereignty of God so she was good ground to understand what the angel said about her. She was also responsible to carry it out.

God made us like Himself, with the power to choose. When I choose to say yes to what God has said to me that is my agreement that the seed inside of me can now conceive. Mary said yes to God, and received His seed and there was conception.

When you become good ground for the destiny of God to be fulfilled through your life, you no longer define yourself according to how you see yourself. You define yourself according to how the Almighty sees you.

When God has a message for you

The word "angel" means message, or "messenger." When God has a message for you, He can send an angel or He can just send words. Words, when God speaks them, have the power to bring into being something from the realm of the spirit that we see manifested in the realm of the flesh. He created the world as we know it by His words.

Jesus said that *"the words that I speak unto you, they are spirit, and they are life."*[10]

When you receive words from God by the Holy Ghost, those words come into your being and we are defined by God's

___

[10] John 6:63 KJV.

78

words instead of the words of the people in your life or even your own thoughts. His words change you into His image, if you receive them into your spirit. You become a manifestation of the words of God at another level. You come to a place where you are able to continually receive seed.

When you don't understand you can still yield to God

As Jesus' momma, Mary was the first human being with the opportunity to make her Son a King over the whole earth. Every president is some momma's boy. Every governor is some momma's son or daughter. When you see a lawyer, doctor, or wealthy businessman, who was the first one who nursed him, spoke into her life, and oversaw his upbringing? Who first dressed him, carried her, and taught him?

Many fathers participate in the lives of their children, but in most cases the life substance that children live off first comes from their mommas. This comes both physically, as they nurse, and also spiritually, as mothers speak into and define their children.

Mary was given the charge of sowing into Jesus on a physical level what Jesus was to become. She was trusted by God because she had faith to receive her assignments and obedience to carry them out with the help of the Holy Ghost.

> *"And the angel answered and said unto her, The Holy Ghost shall come upon thee, and the power of the Highest shall overshadow thee: therefore also that holy thing which shall be born of thee shall be called the Son of God."[11]*

Mary was called into something she didn't understand. We would like to understand God, but in the end, when we move beyond our need to understand everything with our natural mind into a state of yielding, then we can receive the spiritual seed that takes us into the eternal realm with God.

---

[11] Luke 1:35 KJV.

What is in you that can endure to eternity?

The angel said, *"And of his Kingdom there shall be no end."*[12] Jesus' reign will last through all eternity. His rule and reign *in you* will also last forever.

When you leave this world, you will take something with you. You won't take money and material possessions, because they have no value in Heaven, but you will take with you everything that you have acquired from the eternal realm.

Which things in your life will never end? What part of your thinking can be transferred into the next world? What words that you speak are eternal words that came from God by the Holy Ghost? What do you talk about now that you could talk about in Heaven?

If you have not become yielded to the Holy Ghost at the same level as Mary, can you seek God until He comes?

> *"Plant the good seeds of righteousness, and you will harvest a crop of love. Plow up the hard ground of your hearts, for now is the time to seek the LORD, that he may come and shower righteousness upon you."*[13]

---

[12] Luke 1:33 KJV.
[13] Hosea 10:12 NLT.

5

MY FRIEND CAME TO
JESUS' BAPTISM

*"Then Jesus came from Galilee to John at the
Jordan to be baptized by him. And John tried
to prevent Him, saying, 'I need to be baptized
by You, and are You coming to me?'*
*"But Jesus answered and said to him, 'Permit
it to be so now, for thus it is fitting for us to
fulfill all righteousness.' Then he allowed Him.*

*"When He had been baptized,
Jesus came up immediately from the water;
and behold, the heavens were opened to Him,
and
He saw the Spirit of God descending like a
dove and alighting upon Him. And suddenly
a voice came from heaven, saying, 'This is
My beloved Son, in whom I am well
pleased.'"[1]*

When Jesus came to John the Baptist and submitted Himself to water baptism, His Friend was there. His Father was there. Our God—Father, Son, and Holy

---

[1] Matthew 3:13-17 NKJV.

Ghost—the Three-in-One, celebrated that great moment in the history of the world.

Water baptism represents a volitional decision to go down in humility and acknowledge your weaknesses and your need for God. Jesus started His public ministry by going down.

In His baptism, Jesus carried us down into the water to be washed from the pollution of sin. That is the death/life principle. He pictured dying to Himself on our behalf so that we might live.

John the Baptist called men to repent and Jesus came

John was a man, a messenger from God sent to prepare hearts for Jesus Christ by calling people to repent of their sins. Although Jesus was sinless and had no need for the baptism of repentance that John preached, while Jesus was on the earth He carried upon Himself the weight of *our* sins. We deserved to be punished for our rebellion and sin, but Jesus took the full weight of our punishment upon Himself.

Isaiah prophesied that this would happen long before Jesus was born and He described how people would misunderstand it.

> *"Yet it was our weaknesses he carried;*
> > *it was our sorrows that weighed him down.*
> *And we thought his troubles were a punishment from God,*
> > *a punishment for his own sins!*
> *But he was pierced for our rebellion,*
> > *crushed for our sins.*
> *He was beaten so we could be whole.*
> > *He was whipped so we could be healed."[2]*

---

[2] Isaiah 53:4-5 NLT.

HOW JOHN THE BAPTIST PREPARED THE WAY FOR JESUS

Before John the Baptist was born, he already had the Holy Ghost as his Friend while he was in his mother's womb.

Before John was conceived, the angel Gabriel came to his father Zechariah, a priest in Israel, as he was ministering in the temple and told him he would have a son. Zechariah and his wife Elizabeth had been unable to conceive but Gabriel told him that a miracle would happen in his old age. He would have a son with a great mission to prepare the way for the coming of the Lord. His son John would become a Nazarite who did not touch wine or other alcohol. He would already be filled with the Holy Ghost when he was born. Gabriel said:

> *"God has heard your prayer. Your wife, Elizabeth, will give you a son, and you are to name him John. You will have great joy and gladness, and many will rejoice at his birth, for he will be great in the eyes of the Lord. He must never touch wine or other alcoholic drinks. He will be filled with the Holy Spirit, even before his birth. And he will turn many Israelites to the Lord their God. He will be a man with the spirit and power of Elijah. He will prepare the people for the coming of the Lord. He will turn the hearts of the fathers to their children, and he will cause those who are rebellious to accept the wisdom of the godly."[3]*

John prepared for Jesus by calling people to repentance

The angel Gabriel had said to Zechariah, *"He will prepare the people for the coming of the Lord."*[4] When John the Baptist became a man, he prepared the way for Jesus by calling people to repent of their sins because the Kingdom of Heaven was near. He did not compromise with the people of Judea and Samaria. He showed no favoritism to leaders. He

---

[3] Luke 1:13-17 NLT.
[4] Luke 1:17 NLT.

told everyone, *"Repent of your sins and turn to God, for the Kingdom of Heaven is near."*[5]

> *"He was in the wilderness and preached that people should be baptized to show that they had repented of their sins and turned to God to be forgiven. All of Judea, including all the people of Jerusalem, went out to see and hear John. And when they confessed their sins, he baptized them in the Jordan River."*[6]

"Repent" means an inner change of mind resulting in an outward turning around. They not only had to repent. They had to turn around and go a different way—not only in ways that people could see but also inwardly in ways that only God could see.

> *"When the crowds came to John for baptism, he said, 'You brood of snakes! Who warned you to flee God's coming wrath? Prove by the way you live that you have repented of your sins and turned to God.'"*[7]

In preparation for Jesus, John preached that they had to change their minds about everything—how they lived, how they thought, how they talked—every aspect. He said, *"And now also the axe is laid unto the root of the trees."*[8] Whatever your tree was growing on, whatever root system it had before, that old root system has to be dug up and thrown away.

> *"Even now the ax of God's judgment is poised, ready to sever the roots of the trees. Yes, every tree that does not produce good fruit will be chopped down and thrown into the fire."*[9]

---

[5] Matthew 3:2 NLT.
[6] Mark 1:4-5 NLT.
[7] Luke 3:7-8 NLT.
[8] Matthew 3:10 KJV.
[9] Matthew 3:10 NLT.

John prepared by preaching the Kingdom of Heaven

"In those days John the Baptist came to the Judean wilderness and began preaching. His message was, 'Repent of your sins and turn to God, for the Kingdom of Heaven is near.' The prophet Isaiah was speaking about John when he said,

> *"'He is a voice shouting in the wilderness,*
> *"'Prepare the way for the Lord's coming!*
> *Clear the road for him!'"[10]*

John was not only cleaning up the past sins of the people. He was also directing them to see the potential for their future change once they had repented. When you repent, a new seed is planted in you of the Kingdom of Heaven. Ever since Jesus was resurrected, everyone who repents, receives Jesus as Savior, and is baptized in the Holy Ghost has the Holy Ghost. That is the new tree that is growing. This is not just a mental treatise but a living, inner reality. It is the emanating force of the power of God brought by your Friend, the Holy Ghost.

FATHER, SON, AND HOLY GHOST AT JESUS' BAPTISM

When Jesus was baptized, the Father's voice came from heaven and the Holy Ghost became visible in bodily form as a dove.

"One day when the crowds were being baptized, Jesus himself was baptized. As he was praying, the heavens opened, and the Holy Spirit, in bodily form, descended on him like a dove. And a voice from heaven said, 'You are my dearly loved Son, and you bring me great joy.'"[11]

---

[10] Matthew 3:1-3 NLT.
[11] Luke 3:21-22 NLT.

That was a tangible manifestation of all three members of the Godhead together as Father, Son, and Holy Ghost, rejoicing as Jesus humbled Himself to fulfill the Law.

The Father was well pleased because He saw that when Jesus came up out of the water he immediately began to pray.

Jesus, the last Adam, went back and succeeded where the first Adam failed. When Adam sinned in the Garden, He ran from God, but when Jesus carried our sins in baptism, He didn't run *from* God. He ran *to* God by praying. The first Adam tried to save his life but the last Adam came to lose His life. Jesus committed no sin but He bore our sins for us.

This was a powerful moment when Jesus, Who committed no sin, committed Himself to the Father's judgment.

"For to this you were called, because Christ also suffered for us, leaving us an example, that you should follow His steps:

" 'Who committed no sin,
nor was deceit found in His mouth;'

"who, when He was reviled, did not revile in return; when He suffered, He did not threaten, but committed Himself to Him who judges righteously; who Himself bore our sins in His own body on the tree, that we, having died to sins, might live for righteousness—by whose stripes you were healed."[12]

BELIEVE, BE BAPTIZED, AND RECEIVE THE HOLY GHOST

The word "baptize" (Greek *baptizo*) means to immerse, to submerge, to fully cover over. Water baptism is an outward sign that you have died to your old life and your old nature. It is a natural demonstration of your spiritual immersion in God when your sins are washed away.

---

[12] 1 Peter 2:21-24 NKJV.

Baptism follows belief

When Jesus gave the disciples His final commandments in the Great Commission, He said that baptism follows belief and Holy Ghost signs follow baptism.

> *"And he said unto them, Go ye into all the world, and preach the gospel to every creature. He that believeth and is baptized shall be saved; but he that believeth not shall be damned. And these signs shall follow them that believe; In my name shall they cast out devils; they shall speak with new tongues; They shall take up serpents; and if they drink any deadly thing, it shall not hurt them; they shall lay hands on the sick, and they shall recover."[13]*

At Pentecost when Peter preached to the people, they were convicted of sin and asked him what they should do. He said to repent, turn to God, and be baptized and they would receive the gift of the Holy Ghost.

> *"Peter's words pierced their hearts, and they said to him and to the other apostles, 'Brothers, what should we do?'*
> *"Peter replied, 'Each of you must repent of your sins and turn to God, and be baptized in the name of Jesus Christ for the forgiveness of your sins. Then you will receive the gift of the Holy Spirit.'"[14]*

When you go down in water baptism, you identify with the death and burial of Christ. When you come up, you identify with Jesus' resurrection. You walk in newness of life with your Friend Who raised Jesus from the dead!

---

[13] Mark 16:15-18 KJV.
[14] Acts 2:37-38 NLT.

"For you were buried with Christ when you were baptized. And with him you were raised to new life because you trusted the mighty power of God, who raised Christ from the dead."[15]

HOW THIS RELATES TO YOU

Ask your Friend to help you to go down in humility and repent of every known sin. Tell the Lord, "I surrender to you. I am a living sacrifice. I choose to do what You have chosen for me. I choose to die to my own desires so that I can live anew in the power of the Holy Ghost."

Four baptisms of Christians who follow Jesus

- Baptism into Christ—surrender
- Baptism in water—repentance
- Baptism in the Holy Ghost—empowerment
- Baptism of suffering—establishment

Paul pleaded with Christians to see this:

"I beseech you therefore, brethren, by the mercies of God, that ye present your bodies a living sacrifice, holy, acceptable unto God, which is your reasonable service. And be not conformed to this world: but be ye transformed by the renewing of your mind, that ye may prove what is that good, and acceptable, and perfect, will of God."[16]

Paul knew that it would bring a transformation and then the will of God could be fulfilled in our lives.

---

[15] Colossians 2:12 NLT.
[16] Romans 12:1-2 KJV.

"For we died and were buried with Christ by baptism. And just as Christ was raised from the dead by the glorious power of the Father, now we also may live new lives.

"Since we have been united with him in his death, we will also be raised to life as he was. We know that our old sinful selves were crucified with Christ so that sin might lose its power in our lives. We are no longer slaves to sin. For when we died with Christ we were set free from the power of sin. And since we died with Christ, we know we will also live with him. "[17]

Filled with the Holy Ghost, then tempted by the devil

After Jesus was baptized, He was full of the Holy Ghost.[18] The Gospel of Luke records that He was then led by the Spirit into the wilderness where He fasted for 40 days and was tempted by the devil. Mark's Gospel uses even stronger language than Luke. Mark says that our Friend *drove* Jesus into the wilderness.

"And immediately the Spirit driveth him into the wilderness. "[19]

The Greek word for "driveth" is *ekballo*[20] which means to eject, thrust, or send away. Holy Ghost thrust Jesus from that great moment of His baptism into a wilderness experience where He was tested in three areas—the lust of the flesh, the lust of the eyes, and the pride of life.[21] Those were the three tests that the first Adam failed. Jesus, the last Adam, passed them. He never sinned.

---

[17] Romans 6:4-7 NLT.
[18] See Luke 4:1.
[19] Mark 1:12 KJV.
[20] Strong's Concordance of the New Testament #1544.
[21] See 1 John 2:16.

Satan tempted Jesus to disobey His Father—or at least not to obey Him fully—but He refused to yield.

Are you willing to yield to God and refuse to yield to Satan? If you have not been baptized since you believed in Jesus as your Savior and Lord, it is time for this death/life principle to be acted upon in your life.

Jesus responded to all of these temptations with the power and authority of the Holy Ghost. When you spend time with your Friend in the Word and gain supernatural strength from prayer and fasting, you can become so full of the Holy Ghost that you can quote the Bible to the devil and he will leave you alone, at least for a season.

Will you do it?

6

MY FRIEND ANOINTED JESUS FOR PUBLIC MINISTRY

*"How God anointed Jesus of Nazareth with the
Holy Ghost and with power: who went about
doing good, and healing all that were
oppressed of the devil;
for God was with him."* [1]

J esus emerged with such power of the Holy Ghost after
defeating Satan's temptations in the wilderness that
everyone began talking about Him. Positive reports about
Him began to circulate all over Galilee.[2]

> *"Then Jesus returned to Galilee, filled with the Holy
> Spirit's power."* [3]

Between the time He entered the wilderness *full of the
Spirit* and emerged *in the power of the Spirit,* He had exercised
His authority over the devil with the Word of God and had
proven that the devil is not a worthy foe—for Him or for us.

---

[1] Acts 10:38 KJV.
[2] See Luke 4:14 KJV.
[3] Luke 4:14 NLT.

PUBLIC LAUNCH OF JESUS' MINISTRY

When Jesus returned to the synagogue in His hometown of Nazareth, everyone had heard the reports and they were waiting to see what He would do. The Bible says that Jesus stood up to read aloud from the Scriptures, *"as was his custom,"*[4] then turned to Isaiah 61.

> *" 'The Spirit of the LORD . . . hath anointed me to preach the gospel to the poor.*[5]
> *" 'He has sent me to proclaim that captives will be released,*
> *" 'That the blind will see,*
> *" 'that the oppressed will be set free,*
> *" 'and that the time of the Lord's favor has come.*[6]
> *"He rolled up the scroll, handed it back to the attendant, and sat down."*[7]

Next came the historic moment in time when Jesus made His official announcement.

> *"All eyes in the synagogue looked at him intently. Then he began to speak to them.*
> *" 'The Scripture you've just heard has been fulfilled this very day!' "*[8]

With that word, Jesus launched His public ministry and also acknowledged the vital role of my Friend in anointing Him to preach the Gospel.

However, something else was also launched—a violent wave of rejection of His call. Luke says:

---

[4] Luke 4:16 KJV.
[5] Luke 4:18 KJV.
[6] Luke 4:18-19 NLT.
[7] Luke 4:20 NLT.
[8] Luke 4:21 NLT.

"And all they in the synagogue, when they heard these things, were filled with wrath."[9]

Notice the inclusive word "all." *All* who were there rejected His call. No one in His hometown sided with Jesus. In fact, they were so outraged that they tried to kill Him!

"And rose up, and thrust him out of the city, and led him unto the brow of the hill whereon their city was built, that they might cast him down headlong. But he passing through the midst of them went his way."[10]

Jesus' exaltation was coming, but it was preceded by humiliation. You and I need to learn how to handle both.

When they rejected Him, He had to be certain within Himself that He was living to fulfill the Father's will and not to please the will of man.

In every person's life there is always tension between the forces of self-consciousness, the tyranny of the masses (what other people think), and doing the will of God as you are led by my Friend, Holy Ghost. However, Jesus never yielded to the masses. He had another agenda—a powerful ministry of healing, deliverance, and doing good deeds under the anointing.

Jesus, the Anointed One

Jesus Christ means Jesus, the Anointed One. The New Testament Greek word *Chrio* means "to anoint, with a sacred or religious meaning. From this is derived *Christos*, the Anointed One, Christ."[11] Isaiah prophesied His anointing and Jesus proclaimed it that day in the synagogue in his hometown. Holy Ghost had anointed Jesus to fulfill the will of God.

---

[9] Luke 4:28 KJV.
[10] Luke 4:29-30 KJV.
[11] *Hebrew-Greek Key Word Study Bible, King James Version*, Spiros Zodhiates, ed. (Chattanooga, TN: AMG Publishers, 1991), s.v. "5548 *Chrio*."

HOLY GHOST ANOINTING TO HEAL AND DELIVER

Jesus was anointed with the power to do good and heal those who are held captive by the devil. So are we. Holy Ghost is the instrument. When you are anointed with the Holy Ghost and power, your self-life is dead. Jesus lives in you. When He is with you, you are empowered to do good and heal all who are oppressed of the devil.

> *"How God anointed Jesus of Nazareth with the Holy Ghost and with power: who went about doing good, and healing all that were oppressed of the devil; for God was with him."*[12]

Jesus is our solution and makes us the solution for others

> *"And these signs shall follow them that believe; In my name shall they cast out devils; they shall speak with new tongues; They shall take up serpents; and if they drink any deadly thing, it shall not hurt them; they shall lay hands on the sick, and they shall recover."*[13]

The first part of Isaiah 61 that Jesus read in the synagogue deals with deliverance. We are sad, brokenhearted, held captive by sin or circumstances, mourning, full of heaviness. *Jesus has all power to be our solution.* The second part of Isaiah 61 that He read says that Jesus empowers us to minister deliverance to others. *Jesus has all power to make us the solution.*

Here are some of the solutions of healing and deliverance that Holy Ghost empowers us to do in Jesus' name:

- The solution of unity for the divided
- The solution of deliverance for prisoners
- The solution of restoration for the inner cities

---

[12] Acts 10:38 KJV.
[13] Mark 16:17-18 KJV.

- The solution of healing for the sick
- The solution of release for the oppressed
- The solution of courage for the fearful

The solution of unity for the divided

The anointing unifies the whole body of Christ. When each one of us is anointed, all of us are anointed in a corporate unity. Everyone is needed—not only needed but also important. As a matter of fact, there is lack in the body until you step out. There are certain things that are not being supplied until you respond. The anointing oil of Psalm 133 that flowed over the robe of Aaron spoke of the blessing of unity.

> *"Behold, how good and how pleasant* it is *for brethren to dwell together in unity!*
> It is *like the precious ointment upon the head, that ran down upon the beard,* even *Aaron's beard: that went down to the skirts of his garments;*
> *As the dew of Hermon,* and as the dew *that descended upon the mountains of Zion: for there the* LORD *commanded the blessing, even life for evermore."[14]*

When Paul described the gifts of the Holy Ghost in 1 Corinthians 12-14, he emphasized unity.

> *"Yes, the body has many different parts, not just one part. If the foot says, 'I am not a part of the body because I am not a hand' that does not make it any less a part of the body. And if the ear says, 'I am not part of the body because I am not an eye,' would that make it any less a part of the body? If the whole body were an eye, how would you hear? Or if your whole body were an ear, how would you smell anything?"[15]*

---

[14] Psalm 133:1-3 KJV.
[15] 1 Corinthians 12:14-17 NLT.

The solution of deliverance for prisoners

People are not delivered in our prison systems when the focus is only punitive. Prisoners need to be saved and filled with the Holy Ghost to move them from being need-based to being empowered to deliver others. We could decrease recidivism if we empowered prisoners to be saved and become ministers instead of brokenhearted captives. They can become trees of righteousness—people of prayer and good deeds.

> *"To appoint unto them that mourn in Zion, to give unto them beauty for ashes, the oil of joy for mourning, the garment of praise for the spirit of heaviness; that they might be called trees of righteousness, the planting of the LORD, that he might be glorified."[16]*

The solution of restoration for the inner cities

When Holy Ghost empowers you, you can rebuild desolate places and repair ruined cities to the glory of God.

> *"And they shall build the old wastes, they shall raise up the former desolations, and they shall repair the waste cities, the desolations of many generations."[17]*

The solution of healing for the sick

When people are sick and their bodies are hurting, we proclaim that Jesus Himself took our infirmities and bore our sicknesses and diseases and with His stripes, we are healed.[18]

> *"Who forgiveth all thine iniquities; who healeth all thy diseases."[19] "I am the LORD that healeth thee."[20]*

---

[16] Isaiah 63:3 KJV.
[17] Isaiah 61:4 KJV.
[18] See Isaiah 53:5 and 1 Peter 2:24.
[19] Psalm 103:3 KJV.

"Beloved, I wish above all things that thou mayest prosper and be in health, even as thy soul prospereth. "[21]

Under the Holy Ghost anointing, you can pray in Jesus' name and release healing. Speak over the sick strength, healing, and wholeness. Say, "Be made whole in every way!" Then thank the Lord and let the glories of God come!

"Is any sick among you? let him call for the elders of the church; and let them pray over him, anointing him with oil in the name of the Lord: And the prayer of faith shall save the sick, and the Lord shall raise him up; and if he have committed sins, they shall be forgiven him. "[22]

The solution of release for those oppressed by the devil

In Jesus' name, you can rebuke every devil, disease, insecurity and mental disorder.

"He sent his word, and healed them, and delivered them from their destructions. "[23]

Release Holy Ghost to move. Rebuke the devourer and command Satan to loose his hold over them, in Jesus' name.

"(For the weapons of our warfare are not carnal, but mighty through God to the pulling down of strong holds;) Casting down imaginations, and every high thing that exalteth itself against the knowledge of God, and bringing into captivity every thought to the obedience of Christ. "[24]

---

[20] Exodus 15:26 KJV.
[21] 3 John 2 KJV.
[22] James 5:14-15 KJV.
[23] Psalm 107:20 KJV.
[24] 2 Corinthians 10:4-5 KJV.

The solution of courage for the fearful

When you are alive in Christ, you are not subject to fears and insecurities. However, we keep raising ourselves from the dead. We are too aware of our inabilities. We don't have enough education. We don't talk well enough. We don't have enough money. We didn't come from a good family. All of those things drag us down unless we remember that we have access by birthright to receive our inheritance as Christians.

> *"For God hath not given us the spirit of fear; but of power, and of love, and of a sound mind."*[25]

HOW THIS RELATES TO YOU

You need to be anointed by the Holy Ghost and even more important—you need to develop a *Friendship* with the Holy Ghost Who anointed Jesus and anoints you. Holy Ghost brings power and prosperity for every ministry in Isaiah 61 and beyond. When He is your Friend, you can take Him somewhere and miracles break out. You see things happening in people and there is no other explanation except that Jesus did it. You were being fooled by the devil and suddenly you wake up.

Holy Ghost works in you through the death of the self-life and the exaltation of Jesus. Death in you and life in Him. He is not trying to use you just as you are. He wants to do a divine makeover. He is trying to use your body as His temple and it is totally His work. That is the way it is in the Kingdom. You can't do anything without your Friend.

When Satan tempts you to set yourself above God and allow pride to empower you instead of listening to your Friend, you can drive him away—not only for your sake but also for the sake of others, just as Jesus defeated Satan for us.

---

[25] 2 Timothy 1:7 KJV.

SATAN THE SNAKE

Jesus was not fooled. You will not be fooled, either, if you are saved in the name of Jesus and filled with the power of your Friend. When you inherit the sin of Adam and follow the devil, death reigns in your body.[26] Lusts consume your thoughts. When you follow Jesus, you put your pride and the devil under your feet.

Pride is of the devil, humility is of the Lord

When Satan showed up in the Bible in Genesis 3 he succeeded in tempting Adam and his wife to disobey God by calling God a liar.[27] However, when that snake tempted Jesus, He refused. Satan said, "I will . . . set my throne above God's stars." That is his aim but he has no real power to carry it out because he has to come against our Friend, Holy Ghost.

The Lord can reveal His plans to the devil and even write them in a book—the Bible—and still not be threatened by the devil's foolish boasting.

The devil's lifestyle is pride. Pride was his downfall. God cast him out of Heaven because of pride.

> "'How you are fallen from heaven,
>   O shining star, son of the morning!
> You have been thrown down to the earth,
>   you who destroyed the nations of the world.
> For you said to yourself,
>   "I will ascend to heaven and set my throne
>   above God's stars.
> I will preside on the mountain of the gods
>   far away in the north.
> I will climb to the highest heavens
>   and be like the Most High." '"[28]

---

[26] See Romans 5:14.
[27] See Genesis 3:4.
[28] Isaiah 14:12-17 NLT.

Satan masquerades as light but he is dark

Here is what the devil does. The Bible says he masquerades as an angel of light.[29] Everywhere God brings something legitimate, the devil brings a counterfeit.

Your Friend fights the devil and his influence on your life. The devil is a snake working against you. Adam lost his anointing from the snake and Jesus won it back as a worm. When you go down like a worm as Jesus did on the cross and die to yourself, you come alive and Heaven fills your thoughts.

Holy Ghost grieves when we act like snakes

If we are honest, there are many times when we act like snakes. We hold unforgiveness and we're ready to rise up and strike when people walk on us. When people criticize us, we respond with words that have a bite like poison.

As a Christian, I don't want this nature in me because it grieves my Friend.[30] I can't say that I have surrendered to Jesus when I am really in submission to the moods of everyone else. If I react to every negative comment, attitude, or "high look" from someone else by striking back, I am showing that I am a snake who is more concerned with what other people think and say about me than about God's evaluation.

By their words and actions, they have stepped on something that lies coiled inside of me—my old nature of pride. It is the nature of the snake that has inhabited human beings since the Fall.

In the Garden of Eden,[31] Satan fed the pride of the first man and woman by questioning God and making them believe that God was not worthy of their total obedience and that God had not provided everything they needed to meet their needs. They were made in the image of God but the snake reduced them to his level by convincing them to disobey God.

---

[29] See 2 Corinthians 11:14.
[30] See Ephesians 4:30.
[31] See Genesis 2-3.

Overcome the Devil by Holy Ghost Power in You

"Ye are of God, little children, and have
overcome them: because greater is he that is
in you, than he that is in the world."[32]

Some places where you can see Satan's evil nature exposed

- Genesis 3:1-7
- Job Chapters 1-2
- Isaiah 14:12-15
- Ezekiel 28:11-19

Gospel accounts of the devil's failed temptations of Jesus

- Matthew 4:1-11
- Mark 1:12-13
- Luke 4:1-13

Names that describe his infamous nature

- Wicked one (Matthew 13:19)
- The accuser of our brethren (Revelation 12:10)
- Ruler of this world (John 12:31)

When the devil left, Jesus was full of the Holy Ghost's power

- "Then the devil went away."[33]
- "Then Jesus returned to Galilee, filled with the Holy Spirit's power."[34]

The final end of the devil

"Then the devil, who had deceived them, was thrown
into the fiery lake of burning sulfur, joining the beast
and the false prophet. There they will be tormented
day and night forever and ever."[35]

---

[32] 1 John 4:5 KJV.
[33] Matthew 4:11 NLT.
[34] Luke 4:14 NLT.
[35] Revelation 20:10 NLT.

Recognizing counterfeit gifts of the Spirit

You always have the potential to regress in your relationships with God and other people. You have the potential to hear a prophecy and think it is from God when it is a counterfeit from the devil. That's why you need to be on the alert for warnings from your Friend. He will tell you the truth.

"Be sober, be vigilant; because your adversary the devil walks about like a roaring lion, seeking whom he may devour. Resist him, steadfast in the faith, knowing that the same sufferings are experienced by your brotherhood in the world. But may the God of all grace, who called us to His eternal glory by Christ Jesus, after you have suffered a while, perfect, establish, strengthen, and settle you. To Him be the glory and the dominion forever and ever." [36]

In your marriage, you tell yourself it's your spouse's fault but most often it's your pride. You hold on to your anger. You resent being criticized and you rise up and fight back. In time you get fed up with those comments and decide to break covenant and get a divorce. Why? You are listening to the devil and looking at that man or woman instead of asking your Friend to humble you and help you to look honestly at yourself.

Remember the focus. God wants you to look inside and see the pride in your own heart. When people hear you speak or watch your lifestyle, they should witness the character of Christ in you because His nature is growing within you.

When someone prophesies to you and it seems to confirm your bad intentions, ask my Friend for the truth.

"Dear friends, do not believe everyone who claims to speak by the Spirit. You must test them to see if the spirit they have comes from God. For there are many false prophets in the world." [37]

---

[36] 1 Peter 5:8-11 NKJV.
[37] 1 John 4:1 NLT.

7

MY FRIEND RAISED JESUS FROM THE DEAD

"The Spirit of God, who raised Jesus from the dead, lives in you. And just as God raised Christ Jesus from the dead, he will give life to your mortal bodies by this same Spirit living within you."[1]

The primary reason for the darkness in the world, even more than Adam's transgression, is not knowing God and not believing that Jesus Christ rose from the dead.

"Christ died for our sins, just as the Scriptures said. He was buried, and he was raised from the dead on the third day, just as the Scriptures said."[2]

The Bible says that Holy Ghost raised Jesus from the dead![3] My Friend is powerful!

---

[1] Romans 8:11 NLT.
[2] 1 Corinthians 15:3-4 NLT.
[3] See Romans 8:11.

Holy Ghost Who powered Jesus' resurrection is in you

The Bible says that this same Spirit Who raised Jesus from the dead dwells in you when you are saved.

> *"The Spirit of God, who raised Jesus from the dead, lives in you."[4]*

Holy Ghost's resurrection power gives you eternal life. He also gives you authority over your old sinful nature so that it can no longer control you. You are now controlled by your Friend Who lives in you. That is the impact.[5]

> *"But you are not controlled by your sinful nature. You are controlled by the Spirit if you have the Spirit of God living in you."[6]*

You are resurrected to a new life

You are not the same person anymore. Your old nature has passed away and you are a new person.

> *"Therefore if any man be in Christ, he is a new creature: old things are passed away; behold, all things are become new."[7]*

> *"Christ's love controls us. Since we believe that Christ died for all, we also believe that we have all died to our old life. He died for everyone so that those who receive his new life will no longer live for themselves. Instead, they will live for Christ, who died and was raised for them."[8]*

---

[4] Romans 8:11 NLT.
[5] See Romans 8:11.
[6] Romans 8:9 NLT.
[7] 2 Corinthians 5:17 KJV.
[8] 2 Corinthians 5:14-15 NLT.

The light of your resurrection life prevails over darkness

Adam was created with the power to dominate the darkness. When you are born again, the Holy Ghost comes inside to dominate the darkness *in you.* You are both natural and spiritual at the same time. You're both darkness and light—the light of Christ and whatever darkness of the fleshly, Adamic nature still remains. The more you let your Friend take over, the more the light prevails.

The world doesn't believe that someone can walk in the light. The darkness around you can't comprehend what is happening to you when you are born again and filled with the resurrection power of your Friend, Holy Ghost. People don't understand why you are smiling all the time, but you know it is because your faith is alive and your sinful, self-centered nature is dead. You have come alive in newness of life and you know that you have a Friend in need, a Friend indeed.

Eventually, somebody who realizes that this life of yours is real says to you, "You have something that I don't." They see a new reality that exists in you that they have not tapped into yet. That's when you tell them how to receive life through Jesus Christ Who rose from the dead.

THE GREAT FACT OF THE RESURRECTION

Most people who have heard of Jesus believe that He lived historically, but that fact doesn't convert them to Christianity. Just believing that He lived as a Man puts Him in the same category as other great men of history. It doesn't give you a reason to give Him rule over your life.

However, once you understand the reality of the resurrection, that knowledge puts every other religion and every other philosophy under subjection to Christ. No other leader or philosopher—religious or non-religious—was ever raised from the dead and still lives today, except Christ.

Witnesses to Jesus' resurrection

Hundreds of people saw Jesus after He was resurrected from the dead, many of whom were still alive when Paul wrote the epistle of 1 Corinthians.

> *"For I delivered unto you first of all that which I also received, how that Christ died for our sins according to the scriptures; And that he was buried, and that he rose again the third day according to the scriptures: And that he was seen of Cephas, then of the twelve: After that, he was seen of above five hundred brethren at once; of whom the greater part remain unto this present, but some are fallen asleep. After that, he was seen of James; then of all the apostles."[9]*

The first witnesses to His resurrection were the women who went to His tomb.

> *"But very early on Sunday morning the women went to the tomb, taking the spices they had prepared. They found that the stone had been rolled away from the entrance. So they went in, but they didn't find the body of the Lord Jesus. As they stood there puzzled, two men suddenly appeared to them, clothed in dazzling robes.*
> *"The women were terrified and bowed with their faces to the ground. Then the men asked, 'Why are you looking among the dead for someone who is alive? He isn't here! He is risen from the dead! Remember what he told you back in Galilee, that the Son of Man must be betrayed into the hands of sinful men and be crucified, and that he would rise again on the third day.'"[10]*

---

[9] 1 Corinthians 15:3-7 KJV.
[10] Luke 24:1-7 NLT.

In the words of Wesley's great Resurrection hymn:

"Christ, the Lord, is risen today, Alleluia!
Sons of men and angels say, Alleluia!
Raise your joys and triumphs high, Alleluia!
Sing, ye heavens, and earth, reply, Alleluia!"[11]

BY JESUS' BIRTH AND RESURRECTION, GOD IS WITH US

One of the greatest challenges that Christians face is preaching the reality of Christ's resurrection and letting the Holy Ghost prove His reality in the lives of those whom they lead to the Lord. Without Jesus' resurrection, our religion has no eternal value, but He did rise. He is with us!

Isaiah spoke of Immanuel, God with us

"Therefore the Lord himself shall give you a sign;
Behold, a virgin shall conceive, and bear a son, and
shall call his name Immanuel."[12]

Matthew recalled Isaiah's words when Jesus was born

"Behold, a virgin shall be with child, and shall bring
forth a son, and they shall call his name Emmanuel,
which being interpreted is, God with us."[13]

We stand on the reality of the resurrection and Emmanuel, God with us!

---

[11] Charles Wesley, "Christ the Lord Is Risen Today." Online at http://www.cyberhymnal.org/htm/c/t/ctlrisen.htm. Accessed November 2011.
[12] Isaiah 7:14 NLT.
[13] Matthew 1:23 KJV.

"I AM THE RESURRECTION AND THE LIFE"

When Lazarus died, Jesus went to raise him from the dead, but before He did, Jesus said to his sister Martha:

> *"I am the resurrection and the life. He who believes in Me, though he may die, he shall live. And whoever lives and believes in Me shall never die. Do you believe this?"*[14]

Resurrection is a huge issue related to your prayer life and your present faith. Is Christ alive? If He is, He has a direct impact on your life and your quality of life.

> *"For as the Father raises the dead and gives life to them, even so the Son gives life to whom He will."*[15]

Jesus is alive and interceding for you

Is Jesus listening to you? Yes, He is alive in Heaven interceding for you.

> *"Therefore he is able, once and forever, to save those who come to God through him. He lives forever to intercede with God on their behalf."*[16]

If Jesus is alive and He is identified with us as His body and His people, He is not only Lord over us but He is also responsible for us. He is active in our lives. He can quicken those dead in sin with new life because Jesus has life in Himself and He gives it to us by Holy Ghost, our Friend in us.

> *"And you hath he quickened, who were dead in trespasses and sins."*[17]

---

[14] John 11:25-26 NKJV.
[15] John 5:21 NKJV.
[16] Hebrews 7:25 NLT.
[17] Ephesians 2:1 NLT.

"Verily, verily, I say unto you, The hour is coming, and now is, when the dead shall hear the voice of the Son of God: and they that hear shall live. For as the Father hath life in himself; so hath he given to the Son to have life in himself."[18]

WHAT THIS MEANS TO YOU

You have the potential for this resurrection life if you are born again, but in order to be raised to new life you need to yield to God and die to things in your old life. Why would your new life be any different from your old life unless you are truly "crucified with Christ?"[19]

Jesus had to die for our sins before He could be resurrected to bring us new life. We are called to follow His example. You may never have to die in the flesh as a martyr, as Jesus did on the cross, but in order to fulfill the anointing of the Holy Ghost you have to die *to* your flesh. In your flesh you have desires and secret wishes and encumbered relationships with people, places, and things that keep you from yielding to the will of God.

Mary's costly anointing of Jesus for death

Six days before His death on Passover, Jesus went to have dinner in Bethany in the home of Lazarus, whom He had raised from the dead. Mary, the sister of Lazarus and Martha, to whom Jesus had spoken of His resurrection, took a costly jar of perfume and poured it on Jesus' head and anointed His feet, wiping them with her hair. The aroma spread throughout the whole house.

In the same way, we want the aroma of the Lord to be so dominant in us that wherever we go people smell a sweet

---

[18] John 5: 25-26 KJV.
[19] See Galatians 2:20.

aroma, even those in the world. The poor, those captive to drugs, those who have wrong motives can smell the spice in that oil that was poured on Jesus' body.

When Mary anointed Jesus feet, Judas was there also. He was the cheating treasurer among the disciples and he was about to betray Jesus to be crucified, but Judas complained that the perfume should have been sold to give the money to the poor. Jesus replied:

> *"Leave her alone. She did this in preparation for my burial. You will always have the poor among you, but you will not always have me."*[20]

I believe that the greatest challenge to the work of God—to the will of God, to winding up history—is unsurrendered Christians who allowed Jesus to go to the cross but refuse to be led there themselves by my Friend, Holy Ghost.

Revival is not only a question of whether Christians know Jesus but also if they are willing to die, to surrender to His will—even if it means they take on the culture and restore the standards that God set as the Creator of the world.

Society seems to be spiraling downward—not in a positive way toward deeper humility and dependence on God but toward a lifestyle that suits hell better than it seems to suit Heaven. The Church needs to point out sin in the culture and warn of God's judgment. Will you do your part? Have you died to the tyranny of the masses? Can you rise in resurrection life and call others to new life in Christ?

> *"That if thou shalt confess with thy mouth the Lord Jesus, and shalt believe in thine heart <u>that God hath raised him from the dead,</u> thou shalt be saved."*[21]

---

[20] John 12:1-8 NLT.
[21] Romans 10:9 KJV. Emphasis added.

8

My Friend Launched the Church with Power and Miracles

"Go home to thy friends, and tell them how great things the Lord hath done for thee, and hath had compassion on thee." [1]

"And there appeared unto them cloven tongues like as of fire, and it sat upon each of them. And they were all filled with the Holy Ghost, and began to speak with other tongues, as the Spirit gave them utterance." [2]

Jesus gave a vital assignment to the early Church after His Resurrection. He told His disciples to stay in Jerusalem until they received power from on high. As a result, they came together for prayer and reconciliation and conducted business. The Bible says that by the time that Holy Spirit fell at Pentecost, they had the awesome experience of coming into unity. [3] Before the Church launched, God's people were one.

---

[1] Mark 5:19 KJV.
[2] Acts 2:3-4 KJV.
[3] See Acts 1:14.

Pentecost, or the Feast of Weeks, was the second of the three major feasts in the Old Testament that included Passover, Pentecost, and the Feast of Tabernacles. These feasts were times when the Jews made pilgrimages to Jerusalem.

"Pentecost" is the Greek translation of the Hebrew word *Shavuot* or the 50th day. It occurred seven weeks after Passover. The number 50 also represents the Jubilee—every 50th year when all debts were forgiven.[4]

Lamb of God at Passover, Holy Ghost Baptism at Pentecost

Jesus was crucified on Passover[5]—the Lamb of God slain for the sins of the world.[6] Holy Ghost came at Pentecost, releasing the power for the disciples to fulfill Jesus' Great Commission through the Baptism in the Holy Ghost and fire.

> *"And when the day of Pentecost was fully come, they were all with one accord in one place. And suddenly there came a sound from heaven as of a rushing mighty wind, and it filled all the house where they were sitting. And there appeared unto them cloven tongues like as of fire, and it sat upon each of them. And they were all filled with the Holy Ghost, and began to speak with other tongues, as the Spirit gave them utterance."[7]*

> *"They were completely amazed. 'How can this be?' they exclaimed. 'These people are all from Galilee, and yet we hear them speaking in our own native languages!'"[8]*

---

[4] See Leviticus 25.
[5] See Exodus 12 for the sacrifice of the first Passover lamb.
[6] See John 1:29.
[7] Acts 2:1-4 KJV.
[8] Acts 2:7-8 NLT.

They all spoke with tongues

Miraculously, the Bible says that those in the upper room *"were all filled with the Holy Ghost, and began to speak with other tongues, as the Spirit gave them utterance."*[9]They spoke in languages they had never learned. My Friend the Holy Ghost had filled them. Jesus had told them to wait and they waited. They were unified and then the infilling came. People from many nations who were in Jerusalem for Pentecost could understand them in their own native languages.

First reaction of the crowd—scorn

The crowd who heard the disciples speaking in tongues was so deep into intellectualism that they had no clue what was happening. They began to mock the Christians. What was the Christians' response? Did they run and hide from the mockers? Not at all. Now they were all filled with the Holy Ghost. My Friend gave Peter the boldness to preach and all eleven of the other apostles were there backing him. Instead of a retreat by Christians, it became a rout of the devil and 3,000 people were saved. The difference was Holy Ghost, My Friend.

Response of the apostles—boldness!

Peter had never experienced anything like that but he had the discernment to see that this was why Jesus had told them to wait. He saw it as a fulfillment of an Old Testament prophecy by Joel and explained that to the crowd:

> *"They stood there amazed and perplexed. 'What can this mean?' they asked each other.*
> *"But others in the crowd ridiculed them, saying, 'They're just drunk, that's all!'*

---

[9] Acts 2:4.

"Then Peter stepped forward with the eleven other apostles and shouted to the crowd, 'Listen carefully, all of you, fellow Jews and residents of Jerusalem! Make no mistake about this. These people are not drunk, as some of you are assuming. Nine o'clock in the morning is much too early for that. No, what you see was predicted long ago by the prophet Joel:

"'In the last days,' God says,
 'I will pour out my Spirit upon all people.
"Your sons and daughters will prophesy.
 Your young men will see visions,
 and your old men will dream dreams.
"In those days I will pour out my Spirit
 even on my servants—men and women alike—
 and they will prophesy.
"And I will cause wonders in the heavens above
 and signs on the earth below—
 blood and fire and clouds of smoke.
"The sun will become dark,
 and the moon will turn blood red
 before that great and glorious day of the Lord
 arrives.
"But everyone who calls on the name of the Lord
 will be saved.'" [10]

Holy Ghost was now *in* them, not just with or on them

Look at the difference in those apostles compared to the time of Jesus' arrest in the Garden of Gethsemane when they ran away in fear. Holy Ghost was no longer *around them* but *in them;* not working *with them* but *through them.*

---

[10] Acts 2:12-21 NLT.

HOLY GHOST POWER INSIDE TO BE LIKE JESUS

Jesus was a Man in the image of His Father and He developed disciples who would be just like Him on the basis of both precept and practice. That meant that He walked out what He wanted them to become. He shared with them intimate insights that related to the Father. He trusted them with His Father's secrets. He promised them the Holy Ghost Who would validate them as His true disciples even after He had left. He also performed miracles and expected them to do the same.

Jesus chose His 12 disciples and from then on they had a close Friendship with Him for about three and a half years—the time He was here on earth. With His disciples, Jesus set a standard that relationship is more important than responsibility. His relationship with His disciples was a Friend relationship. That was the picture of His 12 men in discipleship under Jesus as Friends.

Jesus' unconditional love

Jesus was an example of the power of forgiveness, such as his challenge to the crowd that was about to stone the woman caught in adultery:

> *"So when they continued asking him, he lifted up himself, and said unto them, He that is without sin among you, let him first cast a stone at her."[11]*

Jesus was also an example of showing unconditional love to children.

> *"When Jesus saw what was happening, he was angry with his disciples. He said to them, 'Let the children come to me. Don't stop them! For the Kingdom of God belongs to those who are like these children.'"[12]*

---

[11] John 8:7 KJV.
[12] Mark 10:14 NLT.

Jesus' miracles spread through the Church

Before Jesus returned to His Father in Heaven, He said that those who believed in Him would do the same works that He had done[13] and He would provide the authority and power. He said, in essence, "If I have called My disciples to love others and take on My responsibilities toward them, I am not going to leave them with all that responsibility unless I give them the power to deal with it the same way I would deal with it." He knew He had to provide us with a Friend Who could empower us to do His miraculous works.

As a Church we date our existence back to Pentecost but as individuals we are descendants of the original disciples. We can do His works if we develop our Friendship with the Holy Ghost just as those disciples had a Friendship with Jesus. We can fulfill the Great Commission if we are baptized in the Holy Ghost. Jesus linked them together.

THE LOVE STANDARD

Jesus said, *"But you will receive power when the Holy Spirit comes upon you. And you will be my witnesses."*[14] Earlier He had said, *"Greater love hath no man than this, that a man lay down his life for his friends."*[15]

When Christians receive power to be "witnesses" we receive power to lay down our lives for others, just as Jesus did. Jesus was using the word "witnesses" in the sacrificial sense—not lightly but speaking of self-sacrifice and possibly even death.

> *". . . and ye shall be witnesses"*[16]
> ["witnesses" is from the Greek word *"martus"* that also means martyr]

---

[13] See John 14:12.
[14] Acts 1:8 NLT.
[15] John 15:13 KJV.
[16] Acts 1:8 KJV.

Jesus' standard of love shown by sacrifice

Jesus called the disciples to a sacrificial standard. The basis of that standard was love—the love that had motivated the Father to send Him,[17] the love that He had from the Father,[18] and therefore the love that He had for His disciples to the point that He was willing to die for them.

Jesus expected us to be like Him. He made this statement about our ability to love others and form covenant friendships:

> *"I am giving you a new commandment: Love one another."[19]*

And he made a comparative analogy:

> *"Just as I have loved you."[20]*

He not only spoke of a love standard. He also demonstrated it in His Friendship with them and asked them to demonstrate it to others. Jesus spoke into them the love standard and the call to live according to that standard as they related to one another.[21] They were called to be close in their personal pilgrimage and called to be examples. Their love would lead others into the will of God. Their love provided the environment for Holy Ghost to come at Pentecost.

Love standard for Holy Ghost Friendship

God is love. Jesus is love. Love is His nature. Love is also the nature of Holy Ghost Friendship. Holy Ghost is love.

What does it take to have Holy Ghost as your Friend? He wants you to absolutely do the will of God and walk in it.

---

[17] See John 3:16.
[18] See John 10:17.
[19] John 13:34 NLT.
[20] John 13:34 NLT.
[21] See John 17.

He wants you to love Jesus and love people. Jesus' disciples would not be His friends if they never paid attention to Him and didn't cultivate their Friendship. The same principle applies to Holy Ghost Friendship.

ACTS—A BOOK OF HOLY GHOST MIRACLES

At Pentecost, the story of Jesus (the four Gospels) now merges with the story of the Holy Ghost. Throughout the book of Acts you read the story of what Holy Ghost did for Jesus' disciples as they lived out what Jesus had taught them. You see how they continually went to God for help, miraculous intervention, and further instructions on how to bring the kingdom of God to earth as it is in heaven.

Spiritual DNA of the Church

Jesus said, *"When I am raised to life again, you will know that I am in my Father, and you are in me, and I am in you."*[22]

Notice the language. *I am in My Father. You are in Me. I am in you.* He is saying that just as He is in His Father, we are in Him. We have the same kind of relationship with Jesus as He has with His Father.

In spiritual terms, when we are in Christ we have the seed of God. We have God's spiritual DNA. We were born first from the corruptible seed of Adam. Now we are born again of an incorruptible seed because of Christ.

> *"Being born again, not of corruptible seed but incorruptible seed by the word of God."*[23]

---

[22] John 14:20 NLT.
[23] 1 Peter1:23 KJV.

When you are born of God, you are spiritual by nature and you can understand spiritual things.

> *"But it was to us that God revealed these things by his Spirit. For his Spirit searches out everything and shows us God's deep secrets. No one can know a person's thoughts except that person's own spirit, and no one can know God's thoughts except God's own Spirit. And we have received God's Spirit (not the world's spirit), so we can know the wonderful things God has freely given us."[24]*

When the Holy Ghost shares God's secrets with you, you can comprehend what He is saying to you.

HOLY GHOST FRIENDSHIP FOR CHURCH LEADERS

In the appointment of the first deacons in the Church, you can see the importance of Holy Ghost Friendship for church leaders. One of the qualifications for leaders was that they should be full of the Spirit and wisdom.

Even in the church's business of benevolence and administrating resources for helping the poor, one of the conditions that must be met was that the Holy Ghost would be the Friend of those men whom they chose as leaders.

> *"So the Twelve called a meeting of all the believers. They said, 'We apostles should spend our time teaching the word of God, not running a food program.*
> *"'And so, brothers, select seven men who are well respected and are full of the Spirit and wisdom. We will give them this responsibility.'"[25]*

---

[24] 1 Corinthians 2:10-12 NLT.
[25] Acts 6:2-3 NLT.

All throughout the book of Acts you see the recurrence of the work of the Holy Ghost changing the lives of leaders as well as the lives of the new believers as they spread the Gospel far and wide. When you are anointed with the Holy Ghost, as Jesus was and as the early disciples were, your Friend stays with you and you carry His presence as you go about doing good and healing all who are oppressed by the devil.[26]

Church leaders who sin have no Holy Ghost Friendship

The opposite is also true. When people go about doing bad things that is an indicator that the Holy Ghost is *not* their Friend. If a person is a bad husband or a bad wife they haven't given themselves over to the Holy Spirit. When pastors, elders, or deacons are in sin they have not developed a Friendship with Holy Ghost.

However, those who have a secret life that God would not approve but then are stirred to confess and repent are returning to the place of accountability where they can build a real Friendship with the Holy Ghost.

> *"Many who became believers confessed their sinful practices. A number of them who had been practicing sorcery brought their incantation books and burned them at a public bonfire. The value of the books was several million dollars. So the message about the Lord spread widely and had a powerful effect."[27]*

CHURCH EMPOWERED FOR GOOD WORKS

Jesus, empowered by the Holy Ghost, His Friend, was an example of the power of going about doing good. The Bible says that Jesus is the Author of our faith. [28]

---

[26] See Acts 10:38.
[27] Acts 19:18-20 NLT.
[28] See Hebrews 12:2.

That simply means that our faith came from Him. He's the Finisher of our faith, which means He's the instrument by which we activate all the things that we do for God. We look to Him as our example.

"Wherefore seeing we also are compassed about with so great a cloud of witnesses, let us lay aside every weight, and the sin which doth so easily beset us, and let us run with patience the race that is set before us, Looking unto Jesus the author and finisher of our faith."[29]

Jesus said to His disciples, "The works that I do shall you do also."

"Verily, verily, I say unto you, He that believeth on me, the works that I do shall he do also; and greater works than these shall he do; because I go unto my Father."[30]

You know when the Scripture says "Verily, verily" that Jesus is emphasizing a point. *We will do His works and we will do greater works.* However, the only way that we will be able to do His works and fully follow His example is by the power of our Friend, the Holy Ghost.

Since God anointed Jesus with the Holy Ghost and power, if we look to Jesus as our example and He was anointed of the Holy Spirit, that means that we ought to be anointed with the Holy Ghost.

If with this anointing Jesus went about doing good, that means that with His anointing we can go about doing good.

Just as Jesus was a good person with that anointing by the Holy Ghost, we can be good people.

---

[29] Hebrews 12:1-2 KJV.
[30] John 14:12 KJV.

Church's powerbase of good people

One of the reasons people are drawn to a church is that they like being around good people. Every born again person is mostly good. I could even say that you're incredibly good.

When you think about the things you've done wrong today they are probably so few that you could count them. How much total activity were you involved in today? How much thinking? How much talking? Did you lie every time a word came out of your mouth today? Did you lust after every person of the opposite sex whom you saw? Did you treat everybody bad that you met? Of course not.

Even while you are in the process of being perfected there is a whole lot of good in you—in your words, in your thoughts, and in your actions. Your Friend, Holy Ghost, is sent to take away all the rest of the bad.

WHAT THIS MEANS TO YOU

When Jesus says, "The works that I do shall you do also," He is saying if you will embrace the Holy Spirit you will have My Spirit. If you think His thoughts, you will have My thoughts. If you speak His words, you will have my words. You will also be able to perform miracles in My name."

The Lord wants to give you the same resources that He had to work with. You're on the same side. It wouldn't be a big deal for God to give you crazy money and you became rich because all He needs to know is that you would look at money the same way He looks at it. Money is just a tool to get something done—to be a blessing to someone and to give God glory.

Jesus' miracle anointing came from compassion

When you have a miracle anointing or a healing anointing, it is not so you can say in some arrogant way, "God is really using me." You would say humbly instead, "Jesus is having compassion through me, making a difference."[31]

When Jesus saw a crowd that had followed Him to a remote area, He had compassion on them and healed their sick.[32] His compassion became the premise by which miracles were multiplied. It was the miracle of feeding 5,000 men and when you include women and children it was potentially 20,000 people. Five loaves and two fish to feed them on the premise of compassion.

If you will let the Lord give you the compassion that comes from Jesus, then you have the potential to work where He worked. The Lord does not waste words and the Bible says that God cannot lie. Therefore, if Jesus says, "The works that I do ye shall do also,"[33] you can do that if you will focus on Him. That takes consecration.

Jesus lived to please His Father and you and I need the same motivation. In other words, we can't have the same manifestation without the same motivation. We can't have the same works without yielding to the Person Who's there to bring the works.

Jesus' good deeds came out of His nature, not instructions

What Jesus did for others came out of His nature. He treated the poor exactly as His Father would treat the poor. He didn't need instructions to know how to treat the poor or talk to a prostitute.

You don't choose what you want to do for yourself when you are in a relationship with the Creator of the whole world. You do what He would do by nature.

I want Holy Ghost to think for me in my mind. I want my Friend's thoughts. I want His discernment. I want to hear the way He hears. I want to talk the way He talks and see what he sees. I want to have His heart. I want Him to embody me. I don't want my Friend to leave me.

---

[31] See Jude 1:22.
[32] See Matthew 14:14.
[33] See John 14:12.

Friendship with Holy Ghost comes from spending time

When you want to develop a Friendship with Holy Ghost, remember that any friendship grows over time. It is not gifting. It is developed.

Take some time every day and say to your Friend, "This is your time." It may be only 15 minutes but that is your Holy Ghost time. You can increase it later. Tell Him, "I want You to get used to having me come to you privately. I want You to become special to me. I want to become special to You. You are here and You will never leave me or forsake me. If our Relationship is not special, it is my fault because You are there all the time."

God loves me. I love Him. I need Him so desperately. This is not about rules. It is about cultivating the Relationship with a Person Who is here.

RESTORING HOLY GHOST FRIENDSHIP TO THE CHURCH

When you have Holy Ghost as your Friend, instead of looking for another move of God, you prepare to move *like God* and bring that move yourself. You see a challenge and you rise to the challenge. You take responsibility for bringing a revolution to the lives of the people whose lives you touch.

Your influence as an individual would be limited but because you have an unlimited God and you live in the realm of eternity, you are thrust into nation-changing situations and you can rise to the challenge.

The Church of Jesus Christ needs a rebirth into the Friendship power of the Holy Ghost. We need to get desperate enough about our immaturity and ineffectiveness that we seek God together until He comes.

SECTION 3.
HOLY GHOST FRIENDSHIP AND YOU

9

MY FRIEND AND YOUR
PERSONAL FAITH

*"And it is impossible to please God without
faith. Anyone who wants to come to him must
believe that God exists and that he rewards
those who sincerely seek him."*[1]

*"In the last day, that great day of the feast,
Jesus stood and cried, saying,
If any man thirst, let him
come unto me, and drink."*[2]

W hen Jesus cried out, *"If any man thirst, let him come
unto me, and drink,"*[3] He was talking to believers
who were crying out for another level of faith.

*"He that believeth on me, as the scripture hath said,
out of his belly shall flow rivers of living water. (But
this spake he of the Spirit, which they that believe on
him should receive: for the Holy Ghost was not yet
given; because that Jesus was not yet glorified.)"*[4]

---

[1] Hebrews 11:6 NLT.
[2] John 7:37 KJV.
[3] John 7:37 KJV.
[4] John 7:38-39 KJV.

This thirst for faith is not created by circumstances. It is a desperate cry for a new level of faith.

GOD VALUES YOU AND HE VALUES YOUR FAITH

You cannot separate the word of faith from the Word of God.

> *"The word is nigh thee, even in thy mouth, and in thy heart: that is, the word of faith, which we preach; That if thou shalt confess with thy mouth the Lord Jesus, and shalt believe in thine heart that God hath raised him from the dead, thou shalt be saved. For with the heart man believeth unto righteousness; and with the mouth confession is made unto salvation."[5]*

> *"So then faith cometh by hearing, and hearing by the word of God."[6]*

> *"God hath dealt to every man the measure of faith."[7]*

Saving faith

Jesus was visiting a Pharisee's house when a local woman known as a sinner came and anointed His feet with expensive ointment, then washed them with her tears. The Pharisee was offended but Jesus commended her faith. He said:

---

[5] Romans 10:8-10 KJV.
[6] Romans 10:17 KJV.
[7] Romans 12:3.

"Thy sins are forgiven. . . . Thy faith hath saved thee; go in peace."[8]

Her faith saved her. Saving faith is faith in Jesus Christ. When your faith is real and your commitment is strong, you don't care if you offend someone. You have to get to Jesus. There is no other way to God—only through Jesus.

"We are made right with God by placing our faith in Jesus Christ. And this is true for everyone who believes, no matter who we are."[9]

Jesus is the Person of Who God is. He is the Word made flesh Who came and dwelt among us.[10] He shows that God is not theory or a definition. He is the Word personalized. You can't think of one good attribute of the Father that Jesus didn't demonstrate. When you think about goodness, you think about Jesus. When you think about love, you think about Jesus. The only way you can miss knowing Jesus is to ignore my Friend Whom Jesus sent to make Him known to us.

Precious faith

When Jesus sees faith, He considers that of great value and worthy of rewards.

". . . your faith is far more precious than mere gold. So when your faith remains strong through many trials, it will bring you much praise and glory and honor on the day when Jesus Christ is revealed to the whole world."[11]

---

[8] Luke 7:47, 50 KJV.
[9] Romans 3:22 NLT.
[10] See John 1:14.
[11] 1 Peter 1:7 NLT.

FAITH—STRONG'S #4102, GREEK *PISTIS*

"Being persuaded, faith, belief.
In general it implies such a knowledge of,
assent to, and confidence in certain divine
truths, especially those of the gospel, as
produces good works."[12]

"Thy faith has saved thee" (Luke 7:50 KJV).

"The real children of Abraham, then, are those who put their faith in God."[13]

Costly faith

When Jesus spoke of those who thirst for faith, He was in Jerusalem for the Feast of Tabernacles, also called the Feast of Shelters. That was one of the three great feasts of the Old Testament—Passover, Pentecost, and Tabernacles. Every feast required costly preparations. You could not take the feast lightly. Each feast had great value in the Hebrew calendar.

Passover commemorated the escape of the Israelites from Egypt when they sacrificed a lamb and smeared the blood on their doorposts to protect them from the death angel that God had to send to kill the firstborn sons of the Egyptians.

The price paid at Jesus' final Passover on earth was a great one—His own life. The person with the value is you.

Jesus is the Lamb slain from the foundation of the world.[14] Through His death, believers in Jesus are saved from dying for their sins. God values you. Jesus died for your sins in your place. One of the tricks of the devil is hiding your true value, but you are unique. God your Father created you and you cannot be replaced.

---

[12] *Webster's 1828 Dictionary*, s.v. "friend." Online at
http://www.webster1828.com/websters1828/definition.aspx?word=Friend. Accessed September 2011.
[13] Galatians 3:7
[14] See Revelation 13:8.

FROM NO FAITH TO THE GOD KIND OF FAITH

Faith is described in different ways in the Bible—no faith, little faith, full faith, great faith, the God kind of faith. Holy Ghost is always active when someone comes to faith in Jesus Christ or their faith grows.

No faith

God is pleased by faith and displeased by no faith! Jesus rebuked His disciples for having no faith when they were together in the boat and a storm arose. He asked:

> *"Why are you afraid? Do you still have no faith?"*[15]

Little faith

In another Gospel account of the storm Jesus rebuked His disciples for little faith. Jesus asked the disciples:

> *"Why are you afraid? You have so little faith!"*
> *Then he got up and rebuked the wind and waves, and*
> *suddenly there was a great calm."*[16]

Jesus expected His disciples to have more than a little faith just based on the works of nature they could see:

> *"And if God cares so wonderfully for wildflowers*
> *that are here today and thrown into the fire tomorrow,*
> *he will certainly care for you.*
> *Why do you have so little faith?"*[17]

---

[15] Mark 4:40.
[16] Matthew 8:26.
[17] Matthew 6:30 NLT. See also Luke 12:28.

Jesus expected Peter to stay in faith after he stepped out of the boat and walked on water, but Peter had only a little faith. When he started to sink, Jesus rebuked him:

> *"Jesus immediately reached out and grabbed him.*
> *'You have so little faith,' Jesus said.*
> *'Why did you doubt me?'"[18]*

When the disciples saw the miracles of the feeding of the 5,000 men and another 4,000 men—plus women and children—that experience only resulted in a little faith for them! Jesus rebuked them for arguing about bringing bread on their journey after they had seen not long before how Jesus had provided all the bread they needed by working a miracle.

> *"Jesus knew what they were saying, so he said,*
> *'You have so little faith! Why are you arguing with*
> *each other about having no bread?'"[19]*

How quickly we forget the great things God does for us! That is why we need more than a little faith. We also need a Friend Who will remind us of what God has said and done.

> *"But the Comforter, which is the Holy Ghost, whom*
> *the Father will send in my name, he shall teach you all*
> *things, and bring all things to your remembrance,*
> *whatsoever I have said unto you."[20]*

Full faith

In the book of Acts, Stephen is singled out as a man full of faith, power, and the Holy Ghost. From the time he was chosen as one of the first deacons until he was killed by a mob incited by Saul (who was later converted to Christ and became known as Paul), Stephen was a man of full faith.

---

[18] Matthew 14:31 NLT.
[19] Matthew 16:8 NLT.
[20] John 14:26 KJV.

"So the Twelve called a meeting of all the believers. They said, 'We apostles should spend our time teaching the word of God, not running a food program. And so, brothers, select seven men who are well respected and are full of the Spirit and wisdom. We will give them this responsibility. Then we apostles can spend our time in prayer and teaching the word.'

"Everyone liked this idea, and they chose the following: Stephen (a man full of faith and the Holy Spirit), Philip, Procorus, Nicanor, Timon, Parmenas, and Nicolas of Antioch (an earlier convert to the Jewish faith)."[21]

Stephen was a servant-leader and he also had the gift of working of miracles. He possessed great wisdom and the ability to preach with conviction. He was so effective at challenging unbelievers that they argued violently with him.

The Bible says that in the midst of the turmoil of a final confrontation with unbelievers, Stephen was full of such faith and peace and so filled with the Holy Ghost that he could see into heaven where Jesus was standing up.

"But he, <u>being full of the Holy Ghost</u>, looked up stedfastly into heaven, and saw the glory of God, and Jesus standing on the right hand of God, And said, Behold, I see the heavens opened, and the Son of man standing on the right hand of God."[22]

The mob was so enraged by his faithfulness to repeat the truth as Holy Ghost revealed it to him and his lack of fear of the crowd that they rushed him and stoned him to death. But as he died, he had enough moral strength and Christ-likeness in his spirit to pray with his last breath for Jesus to forgive them.

"Then they cried out with a loud voice, and stopped their ears, and ran upon him with one accord, And cast

---

[21] Acts 6:2-5 NLT.
[22] Acts 6:55-56 KJV. Emphasis added. Spelling according to original.

*him out of the city, and stoned him: and the witnesses
laid down their clothes at a young man's feet, whose
name was Saul. And they stoned Stephen, calling upon
God, and saying, Lord Jesus, receive my spirit.
And he kneeled down, and cried with a loud voice,
Lord, lay not this sin to their charge.
And when he had said this, he fell asleep.*"[23]

His last words were a cry for God to forgive his
enemies. Could you ever find yourself in a situation like that?
Are you full enough of faith, power, and the Holy Ghost to see
Jesus and with your final breath forgive your enemies?

Do you have anyone in your life who criticizes you and
puts you down whom you should forgive? Is my Friend
stronger inside of you than your desire for revenge, causing
faith and forgiveness to flow in you like a river of living water?

Great faith

Jesus identified an example of great faith when He met
a Roman centurion in Capernaum who came to Him on behalf
of his servant, who was paralyzed and in great pain. When
Jesus agreed to go to the servant and heal him, the officer said
something so remarkable that it provoked Jesus to commend
him for his great faith.

*"But the officer said, 'Lord, I am not worthy to have
you come into my home. Just say the word from where
you are, and my servant will be healed. I know this
because I am under the authority of my superior
officers, and I have authority over my soldiers. I only
need to say, "Go," and they go, or "Come," and they
come. And if I say to my slaves, "Do this," they do
it.'*"[24]

---

[23] Acts 6:57-60 KJV.
[24] Matthew 8:8-9 NLT.

Jesus was amazed. He said:

> *"I have not found so great faith, no, not in Israel."[25]*
> *"Then Jesus said to the Roman officer, 'Go back home.*
> *Because you believed, it has happened.' And the young*
> *servant was healed that same hour."[26]*

You can see three things related to Jesus' view of great faith:

1. He was willing to heal (go where faith exists).
2. He was looking for faith in others.
3. As you believe, so He does an action.

The God kind of faith

The God kind of faith is the kind that Jesus had when He cursed the fig tree and it dried up from the roots. It is the kind of faith that can move mountains simply by speaking, without doubt and without sin. If you believe, you can receive.

> *"The next morning as they were leaving Bethany, Jesus*
> *was hungry. He noticed a fig tree in full leaf a little*
> *way off, so he went over to see if he could find any figs.*
> *But there were only leaves because it was too early in*
> *the season for fruit. Then Jesus said to the tree, 'May*
> *no one ever eat your fruit again!' And the disciples*
> *heard him say it. . . .*
>
> *"The next morning as they passed by the fig*
> *tree he had cursed, the disciples noticed it had*
> *withered from the roots up. Peter remembered what*
> *Jesus had said to the tree on the previous day and*
> *exclaimed, 'Look, Rabbi! The fig tree you cursed has*
> *withered and died!'*
>
> *"Then Jesus said to the disciples, 'Have faith*
> *in God.'"[27]*

---

[25] Matthew 8:10 KJV. See also Luke 9:1-10.
[26] Matthew 8:13 NLT.
[27] Mark 11:12-14, 20-22 NLT.

Jesus said that the God kind of faith can move mountains but it requires that you first forgive others' sins:

> *"I tell you the truth, you can say to this mountain,*
> *'May you be lifted up and thrown into the sea,' and it*
> *will happen. But you must really believe it will happen*
> *and have no doubt in your heart. I tell you, you can*
> *pray for anything, and if you believe that you've*
> *received it, it will be yours. But when you are praying,*
> *first forgive anyone you are holding a*
> *grudge against, so that your Father in heaven*
> *will forgive your sins, too."*[28]

SEVEN FAITH PRACTICES OF A CHRISTIAN

Everything God has in mind for you is good. If someone is sick, of course God can heal him. Sickness keeps you on the pathway to death but Jesus came to give us life.[29]

Here are seven faith practices that you can develop as a Christian that will help you to build a stronger relationship with my Friend, Holy Ghost:

1. Confession (Speaking)
2. Visualization
3. Praise
4. Sowing (Giving)
5. Thought
6. Forgiveness
7. Action

---

[28] Mark 11:23-25 NLT.
[29] See John 10:10.

1. Confession (Speaking)

Remember from the incident with the fig tree[30] the significance of what Jesus *said*. There is great power in words.

> *"Death and life [are] in the power of the tongue: and they that love it shall eat the fruit thereof."[31]*

You can speak healing to someone who has a disease and he will be cured. You can curse sickness and it will dry up like that fig tree because sickness is not of God.

> *"Verily I say unto you, Whatsoever ye shall bind on earth shall be bound in heaven: and whatsoever ye shall loose on earth shall be loosed in heaven."[32]*

You can loose health, prosperity, and joy! You can speak favor to your circumstances. You can decree and declare positive details about your future that will come to pass.

> *"For by thy words thou shalt be justified, and by thy words thou shalt be condemned."[33]*

2. Visualization

> *"Where [there is] no vision, the people perish."[34]*

God gave Abraham a visualization by faith of all that would come to him and his family forever:

> *"And the LORD said unto Abram . . . Lift up now thine eyes, and look from the place where thou art northward, and southward, and eastward, and*

---

[30] See Mark 11.
[31] Proverbs 18:21 KJV.
[32] Matthew 18:18 KJV.
[33] Matthew 12:37 KJV.
[34] Proverbs 29:18 KJV.

westward: For all the land which thou seest, to thee will I give it, and to thy seed for ever."[35]

The centurion mentioned earlier could visualize his servant being healed even though he and Jesus were some distance away. He had such great faith in what Jesus said that he could see something happening before it occurred.

"The centurion answered and said, Lord, I am not worthy that thou shouldest come under my roof: but speak the word only, and my servant shall be healed.

"For I am a man under authority, having soldiers under me: and I say to this man, Go, and he goeth; and to another, Come, and he cometh; and to my servant, Do this, and he doeth it.

"When Jesus heard it, he marvelled, and said to them that followed, Verily I say unto you, I have not found so great faith, no, not in Israel. And I say unto you, That many shall come from the east and west, and shall sit down with Abraham, and Isaac, and Jacob, in the kingdom of heaven. But the children of the kingdom shall be cast out into outer darkness: there shall be weeping and gnashing of teeth. And Jesus said unto the centurion, Go thy way; and as thou hast believed, so be it done unto thee. And his servant was healed in the selfsame hour. [36]

Jesus said that He had not seen any faith greater than that. That was what He had been looking for.

The centurion understood three things about faith:

1. Right attitude
2. Power of words when in right alignment
3. Seeing the end from the beginning (visualization)

---

[35] Genesis 13: 14-15 KJV.
[36] Matthew 8:8-13 KJV. Verse 9 emphasized.

3. Praise

When you praise God, He sees that you have a heart for Him. That gives Him a signal to do something good for you that He already has in His mind.

> *"By him therefore let us offer the sacrifice of praise to God continually, that is, the fruit of [our] lips giving thanks to his name."*[37]

> *"Yet you are holy, enthroned on the praises of Israel."*[38]

Praise is your signal to a holy God that your faith is ready to receive from Him!

4. Sowing (Giving)

Whenever you believe in your own prosperity you are operating within the nature of God. He wants to do something great through you and money is one of the tools He can use for resourcing you and blessing others to whom you give. Your seed creates your future. As long as your gift is in your hand it can never become anything else. But when you sow it, it multiplies into a number you can't count.

> *"Give, and it shall be given unto you; good measure, pressed down, and shaken together, and running over, shall men give into your bosom. For with the same measure that ye mete withal it shall be measured to you again."*[39]

God gave His only Son (seed) and received an uncountable number of sons and daughters (prosperity) as a result.

---

[37] Hebrews 13:15 KJV.
[38] Psalm 22:3 NLT.
[39] Luke 6:38.

"For God so loved the world, that he gave his only begotten Son, that whosoever believeth in him should not perish, but have everlasting life."[40]

There's a lot of preaching about sowing into "good ground" these days. But when God sent Jesus, did He give to good ground? No. He saw sinners and sowed into them to make their ground good.

"For all have sinned, and come short of the glory of God."[41]

You see, God doesn't give to good ground. He gives to make the ground good! Faith in His Son changed the nature of our ground into good ground by the power of His Good Seed.

5. Thought

Your faith depends on your commitment to be a guardian over your thought-life. Paul wrote a final insight to the Christians at Philippi as he concluded, "Finally, brethren," and then urgently challenged them to change their thought-life.

"Finally, brethren, whatsoever things are true, whatsoever things are honest, whatsoever things are just, whatsoever things are pure, whatsoever things are lovely, whatsoever things are of good report; if there be any virtue, and if there be any praise, think on these things. Those things, which ye have both learned, and received, and heard, and seen in me, do: and the God of peace shall be with you."[42]

In a number of other places the Word also speaks of the significance of your thought-life and your need to change the way you think.

---

[40] John 3:16 KJV.
[41] Romans 3:23 KJV.
[42] Philippians 4:8-9 KJV.

- Your mind can be corrupted by the devil.[43]
- Your mind can be too focused on earthly things.[44]
- You can think you know something when you don't.[45]
- You can deceive yourself that you are wise.[46]

A person is not what you see outwardly or what you hear him say but the real person is what he is thinking in his heart, his innermost being.

"For as he thinks in his heart, so is he."[47]

You are made up of spirit, soul (which includes your mind and thoughts), and body.

- With your spirit you have God-consciousness.
- With your soul or mind you have self-consciousness.
- With your body you have world-consciousness.

Your soul or your mind realm was created to take on the image of Jesus when you come to Him in faith. You say "Yes!" to what God has said about you and "No!" to any thought, word or deed that God in Heaven has not confirmed. For example the Word says:

- "But we have the mind of Christ."[48]
- "God . . . always causeth us to triumph in Christ."[49]
- "Therefore be imitators of God, as beloved children."[50]

---

[43] See 2 Corinthians 11:3.
[44] See Colossians 3:2.
[45] See 1 Corinthians 8:2.
[46] See 1 Corinthians 3:18.
[47] Proverbs 23:7 KJV.
[48] 1 Corinthians 2:16 KJV.
[49] 2 Corinthians 2:14 KJV.
[50] Ephesians 5:1 NASB.

You were shaped by God's Word but you have to give consent to the Word on the inside before it takes full effect. In your self-life and the self/soul realm you have to say "Yes!" to God consistently what He has spoken over you.

> *"For Jesus Christ, the Son of God, does not waver between 'Yes' and 'No.' . . . as God's ultimate 'Yes,' he always does what he says."*[51]

6. Forgiveness

An important part of bringing your self-life into alignment with your spirit-life is to be a person of forgiveness. Ask My Friend to help you.

> *"For if ye forgive men their trespasses, your heavenly Father will also forgive you: But if ye forgive not men their trespasses, neither will your Father forgive your trespasses."*[52]

When you have the God kind of faith, you are repentant up to date. You have forgiven those who have wronged you so you can encourage someone else to forgive those who have wronged them. You feed a sinner out of the substance of faith that God is feeding you. God forgives you and you forgive others. God forgives sinners and so do you. He is the God who forgives.

> *"But people are counted as righteous, not because of their work, but because of their faith in God who forgives sinners."*[53]

---

[51] 2 Corinthians 1:19 NLT.
[52] Matthew 6:14-15 KJV.
[53] Romans 4:5 NLT.

7. Action

When Jesus told Peter to let down his nets on the other side of the ship to catch fish, Peter didn't think it would make any difference, but he still took action based on Jesus' words.

> *"And Simon answering said unto him, Master, we have toiled all the night, and have taken nothing: nevertheless at thy word I will let down the net."*[54]

The Bible says that their nets became so full of fish that they almost broke and they had to call for help. Peter was overcome—not only with the abundance of wealth but also by his own sinfulness in the face of such great power.

Another time when Peter and John saw a lame man begging at the Temple Peter said, *"Rise up and walk!"* and when the man took action and stood up he was healed.[55]

When Naaman went to Elisha to be healed of his leprosy, Elisha told him to go and wash in the Jordan and he would be healed. Naaman rejected this action step until others persuaded him to go and then when he acted he was healed.[56]

Faith is not demonstrated when it stays in your mind. You must also show your faith by action steps or works.

> *"What* doth it *profit, my brethren, though a man say he hath faith, and have not works? can faith save him? If a brother or sister be naked, and destitute of daily food, And one of you say unto them, Depart in peace, be* ye *warmed and filled; notwithstanding ye give them not those things which are needful to the body; what* doth it *profit? Even so faith, if it hath not works, is dead, being alone."*[57]

---

[54] Luke 5:5 KJV.
[55] See Acts 3.
[56] See 2 Kings 5.
[57] James 2:14-17 KJV.

WHAT THIS MEANS TO YOU

Have faith in God. The God kind of faith grows in you as you move from faith to faith, grace to grace, strength to strength, and ultimately from glory to glory.

On what level of faith are you operating?

Should you be operating at a higher level based on your level of knowledge? How has your Friendship with Holy Ghost increased your faith?

Is your faith on the production side or the need-based side? Would it increase if you extended forgiveness to anyone?

Based on your commitment, attitude, words, and vision does your faith cause God to rejoice?

Faith of a transformed mind

When I began to see Holy Ghost as my Friend many years ago, my faith grew to levels I had never imagined. I went into my first 40-day fast. I began to see numbers of people delivered by the power of God and many healings—the same spiritual authority that continues in my ministry to this day.

However, the greatest transformation that I recognize in me is the transformation of seeing things by faith from God's viewpoint. I would like to see that happen to you in the coming days as you grow closer to my Friend.

> *"And be not conformed to this world: but be ye transformed by the renewing of your mind, that ye may prove what is that good, and acceptable, and perfect, will of God."*[58]

---

[58] Romans 12:2 KJV.

10

MY FRIEND AND YOUR
PERSONAL ANOINTING

*"The Spirit of the Lord is upon me,
because he hath anointed me to
preach the gospel to the poor."[1]*

*"And it shall come to pass in that day, that his
burden shall be taken away from off thy
shoulder, and his yoke from off thy neck, and
the yoke shall be destroyed
because of the anointing."[2]*

W hen you look at everything that Jesus read from
Isaiah 61 as He announced His public ministry and
then read Acts, you see that the Church is *anointed*
by the Holy Ghost to fulfill the same assignment as Jesus.

The Spirit of the Lord is upon us—*upon you*—because
He has anointed *you* to preach the Gospel to the poor
(spiritually and naturally), to heal the brokenhearted, release
captives, give sight to the blind (spiritually and naturally), free
the oppressed and the bruised, and proclaim that the Lord's
favor has come.[3]

---

[1] Luke 4:16-18 KJV.
[2] Isaiah 10:27 KJV.
[3] See Isaiah 61.

The Anointed One, Christ, extends His anointing to us

The Hebrew and Greek words translated as "anointing" can also be translated as "consecration." Anointing literally means to smear with oil. Kings were consecrated into office and others chosen for special offices were also anointed.

As you recall from Chapter 6, the New Testament Greek word *Christos* means Anointed One, Christ. The Old Testament Hebrew noun *mashiach*[4] also means "anointed one," which gives us the term Messiah.

The Greek word for Christians[5] is *Christianos*[6], derived from *Christos*. It means "little Christ" or, if you will, little anointed one or someone anointed after the anointing of Christ. In 1 Corinthians 12 as Paul discusses the gifts of the Spirit, he says that Holy Ghost baptizes us into one body.

"For by one Spirit are we all baptized into one body."[7]

WHY GOD ANOINTS AND UNIFIES CHRISTIANS

Why are we anointed and joined into one body? To reach those who are economically poor as well as those who are humbly aware of their spiritual poverty and know they need God—the poor in spirit.

Anointed to help the poor

I believe we must not forget that those who are economically poor are the responsibility of the Church of Jesus Christ just like those who need to be born again.

---

[4] Strong's number 4899.
[5] See Acts 11:26 KJV.
[6] Strong's number 5547. Christianos (khris-tee-an-os')
[7] 1 Corinthians 12:12-13 KJV.

"You shall freely open your hand to your brother, to your needy and poor in your land."[8]

"Blessed are *the poor in spirit: for theirs is the kingdom of heaven."*[9]

Jesus said *"when* you give to the poor," not *"if* you give."

"But when you give to the poor, do not let your left hand know what your right hand is doing, so that your giving will be in secret; and your Father who sees what is done in secret will reward you."[10]

"He that hath pity upon the poor lendeth unto the LORD; and that which he hath given will he pay him again."[11]

Anointed for a sweet aroma from your life

The mark of a Christian is to bring "the sweet savor,"[12] or the essence, of Jesus Christ wherever we go. When Mary anointed Jesus feet,[13] He said that she was anointing Him for His death. Ingredients in her aromatic anointing oil had been crushed to bring forth the odor of sweet perfume.

If you let Holy Ghost crush you and break you down so that you get lost in Christ, a sweet aroma will come out of your life through that voluntary humiliation. You will create the aroma of heaven on earth with your Christ-like attitudes.

"But thank God! He has made us his captives and continues to lead us along in Christ's triumphal procession. Now he uses us to spread the knowledge of

---

[8] Deuteronomy 15:11 NASB.
[9] Matthew 5:3 KJV.
[10] Matthew 6:3-4 NASB.
[11] Proverbs 19:17 KJV.
[12] See 2 Corinthians 2:5.
[13] See John 12.

Christ everywhere, like a sweet perfume. Our lives are a Christ-like fragrance rising up to God. But this fragrance is perceived differently by those who are being saved and by those who are perishing. To those who are perishing, we are a dreadful smell of death and doom. But to those who are being saved, we are a life-giving perfume."[14]

Anointed to die to your self-will

"If ye then be risen with Christ, seek those things which are above, where Christ sitteth on the right hand of God. Set your affection on things above, not on things on the earth. For ye are dead, and your life is hid with Christ in God."[15]

Dying to your flesh means that you don't want your own way. You have come to the place where you say as Jesus did in Gethsemane, "Not my will but Thy will be done, Father."[16] Your problem with fulfilling your anointing isn't primarily the devil. Your problem is your pride and self-will.

When I hear preachers and singers say they are anointed, I wonder if they realize that my Friend, Holy Ghost, Who does the anointing, wants them dead! Paul said:

"I am crucified with Christ: nevertheless I live; yet not I, but Christ liveth in me: and the life which I now live in the flesh I live by the faith of the Son of God, who loved me, and gave himself for me."[17]

Before you are anointed like Jesus, you have to die to your flesh so that Jesus can come alive in you. You want your Friend Holy Ghost working in you at a higher level and you want Him to come to stay until you are finished on earth.

---

[14] 2 Corinthians 2:14-16 NLT.
[15] Colossians 3:1-3 KJV.
[16] See Luke 22:42.
[17] Galatians 2:20 KJV.

5 Bitter and Sweet Ingredients of the Holy Anointing Oil of the Apothecary[18]

Myrrh.[19] The finest liquid myrrh, called myrrh of freedom, is collected from the side of a tree where it flows freely. Root words include these meanings—distilling in drops, to trickle, bitter and to make bitter, to be grieved, provoke, vex

Sweet Cinnamon.[20] A sweet spice from bark, aged and then crushed before mixing to produce a strong fragrance.

Sweet Calamus[21] **or Sweet Cane.** Sweet aromatic spice. Root words include these meanings—a reed, erect, a measuring rod, recover, redeem, create, procure, buy, own.

Cassia.[22] A sweet spice. Root words include these meanings—to shrivel up, bend the body in deference, bow down, stoop the head.

Olive Oil. This oil preserved and maintained the fragrances. Oil is often used in Scripture as a symbol of sanctification. Root words include these meanings—grease, richness, fat, fruitful, to shine, brightness, yielding illumination, to be prominent.

Anointed for holiness and consecration

God told Moses how to make a holy anointing oil for sacred use according to a specific prescription. That anointing carried with it certain responsibilities and privileges.

> *"Take thou also unto thee principal spices, of pure myrrh five hundred shekels, and of sweet cinnamon half so much, even two hundred and fifty shekels, and of sweet calamus two hundred and fifty shekels,*

---

[18] See Exodus 30:22-25.
[19] Strong's 4753. Hebrew *more* (mor); or *mowr* (more)
[20] Strong's 7076. Hebrew *qinnamown* (kin-naw-mone').
[21] Strong's 7070 Hebrew *qaneh* (kaw-neh')
[22] Strong's 6916. Hebrew *qiddah* (kid-daw').

"And of cassia five hundred shekels, after the shekel of the sanctuary, and of oil olive an hin:
And thou shalt make it an oil of holy ointment, an ointment compound after the art of the apothecary: it shall be an holy anointing oil."[23]

God told Moses to anoint the Tabernacle, the Ark of the Covenant, the table and utensils, the lampstand and accessories, the incense altar, the altar of burnt offering and utensils, and the washbasin with its stand.

"Consecrate them to make them absolutely holy. After this, whatever touches them will also become holy."[24]

God told Moses to anoint Aaron and his sons to consecrate them as priests. This holy anointing oil would set them apart for prayer and the purposes of God.[25]

"And the LORD spake unto Aaron, Behold, I also have given thee the charge of mine heave offerings of all the hallowed things of the children of Israel; unto thee have I given them by reason of the anointing, and to thy sons, by an ordinance for ever."[26]

These ingredients were a reminder of the Holy Spirit and the aroma of a holy life. When the ingredients were crushed, that was a reminder that Jesus was bruised for our iniquities[27] and His life was a sweet-smelling sacrifice.[28]

---

[23] Exodus 30:23 KJV.
[24] Exodus 30:29 NLT.
[25] See Exodus 30:30-33.
[26] Numbers 18:8 KJV.
[27] See Isaiah 53:5.
[28] See Ephesians 5:2.

DANIEL'S ANOINTING

The prophet Daniel was a man of prayer interceding for his nation of Israel held captive by Babylon. During one of Daniel's times of prayer, he fasted for 21 days. That is the model of the "Daniel's Fast" that we follow in our ministry every year in January to consecrate each new year.

> *"I ate no pleasant bread, neither came flesh nor wine in my mouth, neither did I anoint myself at all, till three whole weeks were fulfilled."[29]*

Notice that it was his custom to anoint himself, because during his fast he abstained from this usual practice. He said he could not anoint himself. Daniel was anointed to intercede for his nation. His power came from pleasing God with his dedication and his fasted lifestyle.

At the end of his 21-day fast, Daniel saw a vision of a man who spoke of the favor of God on Daniel's life:

> *"O Daniel, a man greatly beloved, understand the words that I speak unto thee, and stand upright: for unto thee am I now sent."[30]*

In order to stay in a place of power and favor with God, Daniel had to be intentional about every area of his life.

ANOINTING YOURSELF WITH OIL

Several years ago I looked in the mirror and asked myself, "Do you understand that you must have the right attitude to approach Someone as great as God?"

When I am making contact with God, is Jesus' blood sufficient or could God destroy me in a moment for

---

[29] Daniel 10:3 KJV.
[30] Daniel 10:11 KJV.

approaching Him in the wrong way as He did in the Old Testament to those who displeased Him?

Do I appreciate when I am praying that all of His resources are released to bring to pass again what Jesus began to accomplish on the earth?

Anointing yourself to pray

Prayer is a ministry of the Holy Ghost where divine business is transacted in the name of Jesus. The name of Jesus is so powerful that someday every knee will bow and every tongue will confess that Jesus Christ is Lord.[31]

I considered that since divine business is being transacted when God is moving, would God move for someone like me? God wants to work on my behalf but does God have to work against me because I am out of line? Is God serious while I am just religious?

In that mirror I had a little glimpse of reality. He didn't have to talk to me. He could choose not to. I just knew it was serious right then and there. For a second the fear of God came on me. I said I don't want to be perfunctory about this. I need to be more holy.

From then on, I implemented by the Holy Ghost certain practices including a daily anointing of myself. Every day I anoint myself with oil and consecrate myself to serve the Lord. I want to share this revelation with you.

Anointing yourself for supernatural power

When Jesus said, *"The Spirit of the Lord is upon me because He hath anointed me,"*[32] as I said, the word "anointing" in Greek also means to smear. When you smear yourself daily with anointing oil it reminds you of the supernatural power of God within you. God is able to do

---

[31] See Philippians 2:10-11.
[32] Luke 4:18 KJV.

exceeding abundantly above all that we can ask or think by the power that is at work within us.[33] The anointing represents what is happening to your spirit through the Holy Ghost. This is a natural picture of a spiritual reality that is already true in heaven.

> *"Now unto him that is able to do exceeding abundantly above all that we ask or think, according to the power that worketh in us."[34]*

Anoint yourself as a reminder that God said He would dwell in you. Your body is *"this dwelling where God lives by his Spirit."[35]* There is no telling what God might do through your life. You want every part anointed so that God can sanctify and use you. You anoint yourself daily because you are totally given over to your Friend, Holy Ghost.

Anointing yourself to carry an aroma of holiness

The ingredients of the holy anointing oil were aromatic. The people could tell when Aaron and his sons had been anointed. So I anoint myself every day with a mixture of oil and my cologne as a reminder that the Bible says our lives have an aroma. To some who are not Christian, it smells like a deadly venom and they hate you, as they hated Jesus. To others on the pathway of Christ, your life is a sweet smelling aroma.

Your life is emitting some kind of odor. It is saying something to people who either love being around you or would rather not be around you because you have become a reminder of what they are not living.

---

[33] See Ephesians 3:20.
[34] Ephesians 3:20 KJV.
[35] Ephesians 2:22 NLT.

HOW TO MAKE YOUR OWN AROMATIC ANOINTING OIL

Buy a jar of olive oil and add some of your perfume or cologne. You can give purpose even to your cologne. While you were once using it for your flesh, now you can give it a godly purpose. Ladies, when you take a bath in perfumed water, think of yourself as bathing in the Lord. When that water smells sweet, think of yourself as being drenched in the anointing. You smell good because you're anointed.

> ". . . know ye not that your body is the temple of the Holy Ghost which is in you, which ye have of God, and ye are not your own?"[36]

If you stop by the perfume counter in a department store, they will be glad to charge you a hundred dollars or more for an ounce of perfume so that you can anoint yourself with something that smells good to other people. You may be an unrepentant sinner whose heart stinks up the place but you smell like a rose every day.

You may have learned how to anoint yourself with the devil's perfume but you haven't learned how to anoint yourself with the holy perfume of the anointing of God. You smell good on the outside but on the inside you hardly know the Holy Ghost is there. You are wasting time putting on perfume to change the smell of your flesh. You need to anoint yourself every day so that the aroma of the Spirit comes forth.

Take your bottle of perfume and pour it in some olive oil until it starts smelling good, then sanctify it. Then when you put on your cologne and perfume every day you can call that the anointing of God. Ask God for an aroma within that matches your aroma without and even exceeds it. Why should you smell good on the outside and feel terrible on the inside? If you are depressed, discouraged, and hardly have any faith left for your job or people you know, you need a fresh anointing.

---

[36] 1 Corinthians 6:19 KJV.

154

YOUR PERSONAL EIGHTFOLD ANOINTING

When Gabriel, the angel of the Lord, appeared to Mary, he spoke to her what the Lord had said concerning the Child Jesus Who was to come. Mary responded, *"Behold the handmaid of the Lord; be it unto me according to thy word."*[37]

Mary had a hearing ear that was the key to her obedience. She became pregnant with a revelation from God. Jesus came not through human intercourse but through spiritual intercourse. The womb of her spirit was in her ears.

In the womb of a woman, the Church, God wants to conceive children. The spiritual babies of God are conceived when God comes with a word and you have hearing ears. You become impregnated with a vision for evangelism through your ears. You hear the Word of the Lord and you obey.

The reason that many of us are not pregnant with the blessings of God is that we have been hearing things that bring curses instead of blessings. The devil uses the same ear-gate as the Lord. When you listen to music or movies that are full of cursing and ungodly sex, the devil is sowing into you seeds of death and curses. You are a product of what you let into your ear-gate. How can you become like God when TV is the prophet that speaks to your spirit?

Eight parts of your body to be anointed

- Head
- Body
- Ears
- Eyes
- Nose
- Mouth
- Feet
- Hands

---

[37] Luke 1:38 KJV.

Eight is the number for new beginnings and rebirth

Below are statements that you can declare as you
anoint each part and Scriptures to validate these declarations.

Eightfold Anointing—Head

I anoint my head so that I will have the mind of Christ,[38] that
I will mind spiritual things,[39] that I will be transformed by the
renewing of my mind,[40] that my thoughts will be His
thoughts and my ways will be His ways.[41]

Eightfold Anointing—Body

I anoint my body, which is the temple of the Holy Spirit, for I
am not my own. I was bought with a price. Therefore I will
glorify God in my body and in my spirit, which are God's.[42]
My flesh will be dead to sin—the lust of the flesh, the lust of
the eyes, and the pride of life.[43] I will fast and live a fasted
lifestyle.[44]

Eightfold Anointing—Ears

I anoint my ears to hear the voice of God.[45] My ear is the
womb of my spirit where God is speaking to me to conceive
vision.[46] I will become pregnant with the revelation of God. I
will never refuse to hear what is right. I will always hear
what the Spirit says.[47] In the midst of criticism and
condemnation, I will hear only who I am in Christ. [48]

---

[38] See 1 Corinthians 2:16.
[39] See Romans 8:5.
[40] See Romans 12:2; Ephesians 4:23.
[41] See Isaiah 55:8-9.
[42] See 1 Corinthians 6:19-20.
[43] See 1 John 2:16.
[44] See Isaiah 58; Matthew 6:16-18; Mark 2:20.
[45] See John 10:27; Hebrews 3:15.
[46] See Acts 10:3.
[47] See Revelation 2:7.
[48] See Romans 8:1.

Eightfold Anointing—Eyes

I anoint my eyes so that God will open my eyes that I might see. I will focus on what God is doing so that He can take me beyond myself and my circumstances. I anoint my eyes to see Jesus,[49] to see visions from God,[50] to see which spirit comes from God.[51] I anoint my eyes to see how Jesus looks at me.[52] I will not be distracted by what others see but only what God sees for my life.

Eightfold Anointing—Nose

I anoint my nose so that I will have discernment, wisdom, and judgment in my relationships with others and know what is right before the Lord. Christ is made unto me wisdom, and righteousness, and sanctification, and redemption.[53] If I lack wisdom, I will receive it from the Lord.[54]

Eightfold Anointing—Mouth

I anoint my mouth for words of life, because death and life are in the power of the tongue.[55] With my mouth I shall decree a thing, and it shall be established.[56] I will speak no idle words, because Jesus said by my words I will be justified and by my words I will be condemned.[57] I anoint myself so that my words will be acceptable to God.[58] That they will bless and not curse. That I will represent Jesus in what I say, but never *mis*represent Him.[59] That I will speak the Word and live the Word that I speak.[60] That I will pray continually,[61] so that His presence will be always with me.[62]

---

[49] See Hebrews 2:9.
[50] "Your young men will see visions" (Acts 2:17 NLT).
[51] See 1 John 4:1.
[52] See Mark 10:21 KJV.
[53] See 1 Corinthians 1:30.
[54] See James 1:5.
[55] See Proverbs 18:21 KJV.
[56] See Job 22:28 KJV.
[57] See Matthew 12:36-37 KJV.
[58] See Psalm 19:14.
[59] See 2 Corinthians 5:20-21.
[60] See James 2:14.
[61] See 1 Thessalonians 5:17.
[62] See John 15:7.

Eightfold Anointing—Feet

I anoint my feet that I might walk in the Spirit and not in the flesh.[63] I will walk in His footsteps.[64] I will walk with the weight of glory in my life,[65] so that my footsteps might leave an imprint that the generation can follow. I anoint my feet that my walk might be pleasing to God,[66] in lowliness and meekness;[67] that my life might be modeled after;[68] that I would not walk in any place or destiny that is not ordained for me. That my walk and my lifestyle would take me into His perfect will forever.[69]

Eightfold Anointing—Hands

I anoint my hands to lay hands on people to bless them.[70] To lay hands on the sick and they will recover.[71] To anoint kings[72] and the five-fold ministry[73] into office—apostle, prophet, pastor, teacher, and evangelist. To work the works of Him that sent me, while it is day, because when the night comes, no man can work.[74] That my work will bear fruit into eternity.[75]

When I complete my anointing, I say—

I am anointed today to serve God and man, and to represent Jesus to the world! "This is the day which the Lord has made. I will rejoice and be glad in it."[76]

---

[63] See Galatians 5:16.
[64] See 1 Peter 2:21.
[65] See 2 Corinthians 4:17.
[66] See Colossians 1:10.
[67] See Ephesians 4:1-2.
[68] See 2 Thessalonians 3:9.
[69] See Colossians 1:9-10; Hebrews 13:21.
[70] See Deuteronomy 10:8; 2 Samuel 6:20; Romans 12:14.
[71] See Mark 16:18.
[72] See 1 Samuel 16:13.
[73] See Ephesians 4:11-12.
[74] See John 9:4.
[75] See Isaiah 37:31; John 15:4-5.
[76] See Psalm 118:24 KJV.

11

MY FRIEND AND YOUR BAPTISM WITH THE HOLY GHOST

"I indeed baptize you with water unto repentance: but he that cometh after me is mightier than I, whose shoes I am not worthy to bear: he shall baptize you with the Holy Ghost, and with fire."[1]

JOHN THE BAPTIST

The Baptism in the Holy Ghost is a gateway into your relationship with our Friend, Holy Ghost, after you are born again and receive Jesus as your Savior and Lord. It is not the relationship, but it is the door you enter to Holy Ghost Friendship.

New way of thinking when Holy Ghost is your Friend

When you are baptized in the Holy Ghost, you are immersed in Him. You are lost in Him. Your deeds are His deeds. Your thoughts and words come from Him. Your greatest goal is to obey Jesus, think like Him, and become like Him.

---

[1] Matthew 3:11 KJV.

"Think about the things of heaven, not the things of earth. For you died to this life, and your real life is hidden with Christ in God."[2]

"Those who are dominated by the sinful nature think about sinful things, but those who are controlled by the Holy Spirit think about things that please the Spirit."[3]

Immersed in the Holy Ghost

John the Baptist prophesied that just as people were immersed in water in his baptism, they would be immersed in the Holy Ghost in Jesus' Baptism.

"I baptize you with water, but he will baptize you with the Holy Spirit!"[4]

Definition of "Baptize"

The Greek word for baptize is *baptizo* [pronounced bap-tid'-zo] meaning to immerse, submerge, or make fully wet. It is a derivative of *bapto* [pronounced bap'-to'] that means "to overwhelm, i.e. cover wholly with a fluid . . . (by implication) to stain (as with dye); dip."[5]

The Baptizer is always Jesus

The Baptism with the Holy Ghost is always mentioned in relationship to Jesus. Jesus baptizes you with the Holy Ghost. He immerses you in the Holy Spirit.

---

[2] Colossians 3:2-3 NLT.
[3] Romans 8:5 NLT.
[4] Mark 1:8 NLT.
[5] Strong's *Concordance*.

JOHN THE BAPTIST'S WORDS IN ALL FOUR GOSPELS

When John the Baptist proclaimed that Jesus would baptize with the Holy Ghost, John's words were recorded in all four Gospels.

Matthew
"I indeed baptize you with water unto repentance: but he that cometh after me is mightier than I, whose shoes I am not worthy to bear: he shall baptize you with the Holy Ghost, and with fire." [6]

Mark
"I baptize you with water, but he will baptize you with the Holy Spirit!" [7]

Luke
"Everyone was expecting the Messiah to come soon, and they were eager to know whether John might be the Messiah. John answered their questions by saying, 'I baptize you with water; but someone is coming soon who is greater than I am—so much greater that I'm not even worthy to be his slave and untie the straps of his sandals. He will baptize you with the Holy Spirit and with fire. He is ready to separate the chaff from the wheat with his winnowing fork. Then he will clean up the threshing area, gathering the wheat into his barn but burning the chaff with never-ending fire.'"[8]

John
"Then John testified, 'I saw the Holy Spirit descending like a dove from heaven and resting upon him. I didn't know he was the one, but when God sent me to baptize with water, he told me, "The one on whom you see the Spirit descend and rest is the one who will baptize with the Holy Spirit." I saw this happen to Jesus, so I testify that he is the Chosen One of God.'"[9]

---

[6] Matthew 3:11 KJV.
[7] Mark 1:8 NLT.
[8] Luke 3:15-17 NLT.
[9] John 1:32-34 NLT.

HOW THE HOLY GHOST CAME

- After Jesus' resurrection He breathed on the disciples and said, "Receive the Holy Ghost."[10]
- Before He ascended, He commanded them to wait in Jerusalem until they were baptized in the Holy Ghost.[11]
- On the day of Pentecost the Holy Ghost fell on the believers while they were waiting in the upper room.[12]
- At Pentecost Peter preached to those passing by who witnessed the miraculous coming of the Holy Ghost and then 3,000 accepted Jesus as their Savior.[13]

Baptism of fire

Tongues of fire separated and appeared on each of those assembled at Pentecost.[14] The fire of the Baptism in the Holy Ghost is a purifying fire. It is also a sign of Holy Ghost's guiding presence, like the pillar of fire in the wilderness by which Moses led the Israelites at night.

> *"The Lord went ahead of them. He guided them during the day with a pillar of cloud, and he provided light at night with a pillar of fire. This allowed them to travel by day or by night. And the Lord did not remove the pillar of cloud or pillar of fire from its place in front of the people."[15]*

---

[10] See John 20:22.
[11] See Acts 1:4-5.
[12] See Acts 2.
[13] See Acts 2.
[14] See Acts 2:3.
[15] Exodus 13:21-22 NLT.

HOLY GHOST BAPTISM FOLLOWS CONVERSION

Father, Son, and Holy Ghost do not operate independently. They function in a divine flow. You cannot receive Holy Ghost until you have received Jesus Christ as Savior and been born again. Holy Ghost draws you to Jesus and then Jesus baptizes you in the Holy Ghost. He becomes your Comforter Who leads and guides you into all truth.

Holy Ghost is your Friend Who gave you life in your mother's womb, gave you *new* life when you were born again, and now empowers you to fulfill God's will. Like the apostles, you will not be satisfied to simply win people to Christ. You will also want to pray for them to receive the Baptism in the Holy Ghost with visible miracles and manifestations.

> *"When the apostles in Jerusalem heard that the people of Samaria had accepted God's message, they sent Peter and John there. As soon as they arrived, they prayed for these new believers to receive the Holy Spirit. The Holy Spirit had not yet come upon any of them, for they had only been baptized in the name of the Lord Jesus. Then Peter and John laid their hands upon these believers, and they received the Holy Spirit."[16]*

Gifts of the Holy Ghost

- Word of wisdom
- Word of knowledge
- Faith
- Healing
- Working of miracles
- Prophecy
- Discerning of spirits
- Speaking in unknown tongues
- Interpretation of tongues[17]

---

[16] Acts 8:12-17 NLT. See also Acts 19:1-6.
[17] See 1 Corinthians 12:7-10.

ENDORSEMENTS OF THE BAPTISM WITH THE HOLY GHOST

Jesus
"And, being assembled together with them, commanded them that they should not depart from Jerusalem, but wait for the promise of the Father, which, saith he, ye have heard of me. For John truly baptized with water; but ye shall be baptized with the Holy Ghost."[18]

John the Baptist
". . . when God sent me to baptize with water, he told me, 'The one on whom you see the Spirit descend and rest is the one who will baptize with the Holy Spirit.' I saw this happen to Jesus, so I testify that he is the Chosen One of God."[19]

Apostle Paul
"Now there are diversities of gifts, but the same Spirit. And there are differences of administrations, but the same Lord. And there are diversities of operations, but it is the same God which worketh all in all. But the manifestation of the Spirit is given to every man to profit withal. For to one is given by the Spirit the word of wisdom; to another the word of knowledge by the same Spirit; To another faith by the same Spirit; to another the gifts of healing by the same Spirit; To another the working of miracles; to another prophecy; to another discerning of spirits; to another divers kinds of tongues; to another the interpretation of tongues: But all these worketh that one and the selfsame Spirit, dividing to every man severally as he will."[20]

Peter
"When the apostles in Jerusalem heard that the people of Samaria had accepted God's message, they sent Peter and John there. As soon as they arrived, they prayed for these new believers to receive the Holy Spirit. The Holy Spirit had not yet come upon any of them, for they had only been baptized in the name of the Lord Jesus. Then Peter and John laid their hands upon these believers, and they received the Holy Spirit. When Simon saw that the Spirit was given when the apostles laid their hands on people, he offered them money to buy this power."[21]

---

[18] Acts 1:4-5 KJV.
[19] John 1:33-34 NLT.
[20] 1 Corinthians 12:4-11 KJV.
[21] Acts 8:14-18 NLT.

HOLY GHOST BAPTISM—FULFILLMENT OF PROPHECY

At Pentecost, while 120 disciples were tarrying in the upper room in obedience to Jesus' command to wait for the promise of the Father, Holy Ghost fell with the force of a rushing mighty wind and tongues of fire rested on each one. Then they began to speak in languages they had never learned as the Spirit gave them utterance. They were preaching in the actual languages of people from other nations who had come to Jerusalem to celebrate the Jewish feast of Pentecost. They had never been taught those languages. The words came out of their mouths by the power of the Holy Ghost Baptism.

Peter preached to the crowd with explosive impact as he quoted from the prophet Joel. He said that Joel prophesied years before Jesus' birth that the Spirit would come in this way.

> *"But this is that which was spoken by the prophet Joel;*
> *"And it shall come to pass in the last days,*
> *saith God, I will pour out of my Spirit upon all flesh:*
> *and your sons and your daughters shall prophesy, and*
> *your young men shall see visions, and your old men*
> *shall dream dreams:*
> *"And on my servants and on my handmaidens*
> *I will pour out in those days of my Spirit; and they*
> *shall prophesy:*
> *"And I will show wonders in heaven above,*
> *and signs in the earth beneath; blood, and fire, and*
> *vapor of smoke:*
> *"The sun shall be turned into darkness, and*
> *the moon into blood, before that great and notable day*
> *of the Lord come:*
> *"And it shall come to pass, that whosoever*
> *shall call on the name of the Lord shall be saved."[22]*

Only 50 days earlier when Jesus was arrested, Peter had denied that he even knew Jesus, but now he preached to strangers with such power and authority that 3,000 were saved.

---

[22] Acts 2:16-21 KJV. Spelling updated.

"Now when they heard this, they were pricked in their heart, and said unto Peter and to the rest of the apostles, Men and brethren, what shall we do? Then Peter said unto them, Repent, and be baptized every one of you in the name of Jesus Christ for the remission of sins, and ye shall receive the gift of the Holy Ghost."[23]

FAITH-BUILDING EXPERIENCE OF THE GIFT OF TONGUES

When you receive the Holy Ghost and speak in tongues, it is such a supernatural experience that you gain a new appreciation for how close a believer can be to God. When God can change the words that come out of your mouth, you know He is with you in the Person of the Holy Ghost.

We need Holy Ghost power and authority today more than ever. You need a depth of conviction inside that tells you that you are of God and what you want is what God wants. That assurance comes from being baptized in the Holy Ghost and totally given over to God in every way.

Consistently praying in tongues

When you pray daily in the spirit and pray with your understanding, you can maintain constant communion with God through your Friend, Holy Ghost. That is what Paul did:

"Well then, what shall I do? I will pray in the spirit, and I will also pray in words I understand. I will sing in the spirit, and I will also sing in words I understand."[24] "I thank God that I speak in tongues more than any of you."[25]

---

[23] Acts 2:37-38 KJV.
[24] 1 Corinthians 14:15 NLT. Emphasis added.
[25] 1 Corinthians 14:18 NLT. Emphasis added.

In both passages, Paul makes the decision to *pray* and *speak* in tongues. We are to fully benefit from the tongues dimension of our relationship with God!

Caution used in public settings; power achieved in private

Churches where Holy Ghost is released to bring manifestations often differentiate between praying in tongues in your private devotional time and praying in tongues aloud in a public meeting. Paul's admonitions about speaking in tongues in 1 Corinthians 14 appeal for caution only in public settings.

If you are speaking out in a public meeting, Paul says, you should either ask God to give you the interpretation of tongues or expect God to give someone else the interpretation immediately, for the sake of the people. He said it is too disorderly for several different people to speak out messages in tongues that are never interpreted. Nobody listening knows what God is saying to those who are assembled.

> *"For if the trumpet give an uncertain sound, who shall prepare himself to the battle?"*[26]

However, the freedom to pray in tongues privately is a supernatural source of inner strength. The apostle Paul, in addition to saying, *"I thank God, I speak in tongues more than you all,"*[27] also wrote:

> *"He that speaketh in an unknown tongue edifieth himself."*[28]

Edifying yourself means building up yourself. Jude says:

> *"But ye, beloved, building up yourselves on your most holy faith, praying in the Holy Ghost."*[29]

---

[26] 1 Corinthians 14:8 KJV.
[27] 1 Corinthians 14:18 NASB.
[28] 1 Corinthians 14:4 KJV.
[29] Jude 1:20 KJV.

Speaking in tongues influences unbelievers to believe

Paul said that speaking in tongues is a sign for unbelievers.[30] Also, when they hear someone prophesy about them, which may be a direct word from God or a combination of speaking in tongues followed by an interpretation of tongues, this makes a powerful impact on them.

"As they listen, their secret thoughts will be exposed, and they will fall to their knees and worship God, declaring, 'God is truly here among you.'"[31]

Testimony of an Unbelieving Jew a Century Ago

How a skeptic was converted at Azusa Street when Holy Ghost power returned to the Church at the beginning of the 20th century.

"I am a Jew, and I came to this city to investigate this speaking in tongues. No person in this city knows my first or my last name, as I am here under an assumed name. No one in this city knows my occupation, or anything about me. I go to hear preachers for the purpose of taking their sermons apart, and using them in lecturing against the Christian religion.

"This girl, as I entered the room, started speaking in the Hebrew language. She told me my first name and my last name, and she told me why I was in the city and what my occupation was in life, and then she called upon me to repent. She told me things about my life which it would be impossible for any person in this city to know.'

"Then [Mr. McAlister's letter concludes], the man dropped to his knees and cried and prayed as though his heart would break."[32]

---

[30] See 1 Corinthians 14:22.
[31] 1 Corinthians 14: 25 NLT.
[32] John L. Sherrill, *They speak With Other Tongues* (New York: McGraw Hill, 1964), 41,42. Quoted in Vinson Synan, "The Lasting Legacies of the Azusa Street Revival." Online at http://enrichmentjournal.ag.org/200602/200602_142_Legacies.cfm. Accessed October 2011. Used by permission.

KEEP ON ASKING FOR MORE OF THE HOLY GHOST

Jesus said emphatically to us as His believers:

"And I say unto you, Ask, and it shall be given you; seek, and ye shall find; knock, and it shall be opened unto you. For every one that asketh receiveth; and he that seeketh findeth; and to him that knocketh it shall be opened. If a son shall ask bread of any of you that is a father, will he give him a stone? or if he ask a fish, will he for a fish give him a serpent? Or if he shall ask an egg, will he offer him a scorpion? If ye then, being evil, know how to give good gifts unto your children: how much more shall your heavenly Father give the Holy Spirit to them that ask him?"[33]

The New Living Translation of this passage accurately portrays what Jesus said—that those actions of asking, seeking, and knocking are continuous, not one-time occurrences.

"And so I tell you, keep on asking, and you will receive what you ask for. Keep on seeking, and you will find. Keep on knocking, and the door will be opened to you."[34]

You develop your relationship as you pray and keep on asking for more Holy Ghost in your life. This takes time and respectful repetition to show that you have faith for what you are asking. "Yes" is your only expectation!

Remember the word ASK

When you take the first letter in each of the words Ask, Seek, and Knock they spell ASK. As a Christian sold out to the Holy Ghost, you can ASK in prayer from a position of

---

[33] Luke 11:9-13 KJV.
[34] Luke 11:9 NLT.

commitment. God sees by your perseverance that you have invited your Friend into your life to stay. You have not taken something from Him abruptly and then left. You are a real friend. You are developing depth because you keep on building your relationship by asking, seeking, and knocking in a faith dialogue. He's the greatest Friend and comes as a total resource person!

Your prayer language may not come immediately

Some believers ask Jesus to baptize them in the Holy Ghost and speak in tongues as an instant manifestation, but it is not always the case. The disciples' experienced the Baptism with the Holy Ghost and spoke in tongues at Pentecost in a moment of time. However, that moment did not come without effort. They had first sought to obey Jesus and follow Him with commitment and sacrifice.

What do you think it cost them to spend those days in the upper room after Jesus ascended to the Father? They were learning together how to appreciate what God had done by coming into one accord as they waited together.

When the Spirit fell, they were able to speak in tongues but they were also able to preach and win souls to Jesus. From then on, they were able to endure ridicule, persecution, suffering, and even death. Their supernatural connection to the living God through an ongoing Friendship with the Holy Ghost gave them the faith perspective they needed. Those trials were only temporary. They knew that *"what we suffer now is nothing compared to the glory he will reveal to us later."*[35]

When will the gift come and what should you do while you are waiting? Keep seeking God and reading what He said in His Word. Spend time in Christian churches and other Christian environments where expressions of His miracles and manifestations are welcome. Fulfill the Great Commission.

---

[35] Romans 8:18 NLT.

DIFFERENCE BETWEEN CHARISMA AND ANOINTING

Be sure to discern the difference between the charisma (spiritual gifts of 1 Corinthians 12 and 14) and the anointing.

Charisma with substance of the anointing

The true anointing is charisma with substance—a person who is operating in the gifts yet still has the substance of the character of Christ working in depth inside of him. When he speaks, people are changed. When he comes around you, you are changed. His words are accurate.

Devil can counterfeit gifts

The devil can counterfeit the Spirit's gifts. Someone who gives you a prophecy and says it came from God could be lying. You need to try the spirits, the Bible says. You should not act upon a private prophecy from an individual. You need to follow the Bible plus two or three witnesses who can vouch for that word and that person. You need the witness of Scripture and your own relationship with your Friend.

Beware of charisma without character

People who demonstrate the gifts of the Spirit in public places may not necessarily have the character of Christ in their secret life. A charismatic person who seems excited talking about Jesus might be living in secret sin because Holy Ghost is not his Friend. A charismatic Christian without the anointing may be judgmental against those who have not experienced Holy Ghost Baptism even though the Bible says to love one another.

Seal of your relationship with Jesus

"Now he which establisheth us with you in Christ, and hath anointed us, is God; Who hath also sealed us, and given the earnest of the Spirit in our hearts."[36]

"The Spirit is God's guarantee that he will give us the inheritance he promised and that he has purchased us to be his own people. He did this so we would praise and glorify him."[37]

WHAT THIS MEANS TO YOU

You can receive the Baptism in the Holy Ghost when you are born again and your heart is good ground for Him to come and live in you. If your heart is not good ground, ask God to break up the fallow ground in your heart.

"Sow to yourselves in righteousness, reap in mercy; break up your fallow ground: for it is time to seek the LORD, till he come and rain righteousness upon you."[38]

Pray, "Reveal to me any sin in me that would keep the power of my Friend from coming into me and flowing through me to others around me."

Read and meditate on 1 Corinthians Chapters 12, 13, and 14. Review the selected Scriptures from Acts found in Appendix 1 as well as others that you have noted as you have read this book. Remember, Jesus said to ASK for Holy Spirit.

"So if you sinful people know how to give good gifts to your children, how much more will your heavenly Father give the Holy Spirit to those who ask him."[39]

---

[36] 2 Corinthians 1:22-23 KJV.
[37] Ephesians 1:14 NLT. Spelling adapted.
[38] Hosea 10:12 KJV.
[39] Luke 11:13 NLT.

12

MY FRIEND AND YOUR CONSECRATION

"Whoever loves a pure heart and gracious speech will have the king as a friend."[1]

"And one cried unto another, and said, Holy, holy, holy, is the LORD of hosts: the whole earth is full of his glory."[2]

Sometime after my mother was born again, while I was still a child, we moved from Atlantic City to Baltimore. She was a single mom and we didn't have a place to stay so we moved in with the bishop of a local church. However, his moves toward my mother while we were living there could not be characterized as holy. His attitudes were not something that would please my Friend.

The greatest goal that you and I could ever have is pleasing God. In the process, we never know how many people are going to be pleased and their children protected, as well. That takes holiness.

God's nature is holy. Holy Ghost's name reminds us of the holiness of the Lord.

---

[1] Proverbs 22:11 NLT.
[2] Isaiah 6:3 KJV.

"Who is like unto thee, O LORD, among the gods? who is like thee, glorious in holiness, fearful in praises, doing wonders?"[3]

"But thou art holy, O thou that inhabitest the praises of Israel."[4]

"And the four beasts had each of them six wings about him; and they were full of eyes within: and they rest not day and night, saying, Holy, holy, holy, Lord God Almighty, which was, and is, and is to come."[5]

THE FALL OF CHRISTIAN LEADERS

Years ago I knew a Christian leader who had a worldwide television ministry that was filled with signs and wonders. He was selling recordings of his teachings everywhere, yet he came to the place that he had to admit he was not living everything he had taught in his audio library.

A lot of what he taught had not come from his own revelations. He admitted that he had learned his messages from other teachers' books and other men's teachings.

When he was convicted of his sin, he could not teach it any more. He even burned former recordings and started all over again. He began to seek God for his own revelation. He understood that he had to live out sanctification, prayer, and the cross of Jesus based on his own dedication and commitment to Christ and a relationship with God through the Holy Ghost.

Flaky Christians are not the ones whom God will use to do a solid rock work. Jesus doesn't build His church on sand. Pastors who compromise raise people who compromise. If you build a church or ministry on *what God can do for you,* you misunderstand the true focus and emphasis of God. You think that God exists for you rather than that *you exist for God.*

---

[3] Exodus 15:11 KJV.
[4] Psalms 22:3 KJV.
[5] Revelation 4:8 KJV.

This man had the gifts of the Spirit but that was what they were—gifts. The gift says nothing about the one with the gift. It only says something about the One who gave it.

We think that a man who operates in the gifts of the Spirit is such an awesome person that we send him money and read all his books. However, without the gift of discerning of spirits we don't understand when his life and doctrine are wrong until he fails. He needs to get his life together and rededicate himself to Holy Ghost Friendship and oversight by a spiritual dad. In God's sight he is living an unapproved life on the inside.

This man was committed to healings and miracles but he wasn't committed to a personal revelation of God from a devoted Friendship with God.

> ### *God requires that Christian pastors and leaders build upon personal fire, not second-hand smoke.*

Your commitment is exposed by your involvement with Christ. Are you religious or do you have a real relationship with God?

The word "Christian" means "Christ-like." The Bible says in Deuteronomy 8:18 that God gives us power to get wealth so that he might establish his covenant. You may think that God gave you power to get wealth so that you can get another house or another car. In Haggai it says you need to consider your ways.[6] This is not the time for you to build your own house. It is time for you to build the house of the Lord. You are putting your money into bags with holes in it. The holes are not in your checking account. The holes are in your spirit. It leaks. Consequently, your spirit is not flowing in the direction of the Spirit of God.

> *"And be not drunk with wine, wherein is excess; but be filled with the Spirit."*[7]

---

[6] See Haggai 1:5.
[7] Ephesians 5:18 KJV.

Restoring the call to holiness—even to pastors

We need to restore old words to the vocabulary of Christians, words like "holiness" and "consecration." We have lost our understanding of holiness because most of the time we compare ourselves to someone whom we may know who is holy. We have stereotypes of a holy person and we see holiness as something that is not only unattainable but oftentimes unwelcome. We use man-made rules to define every "jot and tittle" of outward holiness, then impose these rules on one another, without ever producing the substance of Christ-like holiness on the inside, in our inner nature.

> *"For such an high priest [Jesus] became us,* who is *holy, harmless, undefiled, separate from sinners, and made higher than the heavens."*[8]

One of the bishops I know well was once associated with a group of pastors who could preach a revival in a church service and then go out together to the bars or a strip-tease show. They smoked and drank and told jokes and wondered why he had a problem with that. These men could not have been friends with Holy Ghost!

God clearly makes a difference between the holy and the profane.[9] Holiness is basically being like God. After you are born again, one of your most importance goals is holiness.

---

[8] Hebrews 7:26 NLT.
[9] See Ezekiel 22:26.

"Don't slip back into your old ways of living to satisfy your own desires. You didn't know any better then. But now you must be holy in everything you do, just as God who chose you is holy. For the Scriptures say, 'You must be holy because I am holy.'"[10]

When your relationship with God centers around the responsiveness of your heart to His holiness, you want to please your Father. Your whole being—your life—becomes an instrument of responsiveness to God—an instrument of worship.

Experiencing the glory of God's holiness

We need to call one another to true holiness. Holiness is manifested in true worship. An experience with the glory of God brings an increasing sensitivity to the Holy Ghost speaking into your life about your change. If legalistic holiness does not bring an increase in your worship, it is not true holiness. You are still using your own measures to get closer to God. You need to seek the Lord without limits in order to experience His holiness.

> *"O sing unto the LORD a new song; for he hath done marvellous things: his right hand, and his holy arm, hath gotten him the victory."*[11]

CONSECRATION BEGINS IN PRAYER

Consecration begins in prayer. God accepts you. You are His beloved, but when you offer yourself to God, be pure in heart. Let Him deal with every shadow that might show up in the light of His holiness as God exposes you. If God isn't

---

[10] 1 Peter 1:14-16 NLT.
[11] Psalms 98:1 KJV.

dealing with you about your dark side, then you know you aren't getting before Him seriously enough. When you get before God He will always be perfecting you, "perfecting holiness in the fear of God."[12]

> *"Therefore, come out from among unbelievers,*
> *and separate yourselves from them, says the Lord.*
> *Don't touch their filthy things,*
> *and I will welcome you.*
> *And I will be your Father,*
> *and you will be my sons and daughters,*
> *says the Lord Almighty."[13]*

Holy Ghost is in you, praying

Jesus could pray effectively for His disciples because He knew them so well. He knew Peter's weakness.

> *"And the Lord said, Simon, Simon, behold, Satan hath desired to have you, that he may sift you as wheat: But I have prayed for thee, that thy faith fail not."[14]*

My Friend Holy Ghost also prays for us in our weaknesses because of His intimate knowledge of us:

> *"And the Holy Spirit helps us in our weakness. For example, we don't know what God wants us to pray for. But the Holy Spirit prays for us with groanings that cannot be expressed in words. And the Father who knows all hearts knows what the Spirit is saying, for the Spirit pleads for us believer in harmony with God's own will."[15]*

---

[12] 2 Corinthians 7:1 KJV.
[13] 2 Corinthians 6:17-18 NLT.
[14] Luke 22:31-32 KJV.
[15] Romans 8:26-27 NLT.

CONSECRATION COMES THROUGH CORRECTION

One of the ways you can tell if you have a wrong spirit is that when you get rebuked you are angry about it. You carry the hurt of the rebuke rather than understanding that correction shows you the way out of spiritual bondage.

God gives us opportunities to become more godly by rebuking us or allowing someone in our lives to rebuke us to the point where we repent. We are not upset about the rebuke but we are rejoicing because we needed to hear the truth.

Your true effectiveness as a child of God relates to your commitment to correction. God has to bring us back to real Christianity so that our lives become awesome and the only explanation is that we must be serving God. We must know Holy Ghost as our Friend!

Allowing the Word to read you

I often think of the words of the late Derek Prince, a great Bible teacher and Christian. He said, "I found that when I was reading the Bible, the Bible was reading me."

When you read the Word, you become the Word inside. The Bible is more than new information. You are eating the substance of God's life and applying it to your life, building a spiritual momentum that carries you to places unknown.

Man looks at the outside, but God looks inside, at the heart. God created Adam's spirit before He built him a body. He always works from the inside out. You are born again on the inside and then He forms your character that is seen on the outside. The more you eat internally, the more you grow in outward works.

Growing up and feeding yourself the Word

In a family, at a certain age babies become old enough for their parents to give them a spoon so they can eat for themselves. Maybe they're making a mess and it's all over the place and you have to clean up the mess, but you know they have to learn to feed themselves before they can grow up.

A lot of Christians can walk, put on their own clothes, and do all kinds of service for the church but they still want somebody else to feed them.

At some point Christians have to say, "I am going to grow up and feed myself my own spiritual food. I will devote my total understanding to God. I will seek help from my Friend, Holy Ghost. I refuse to be limited by religious prejudice, educational training, or what my parents told me, what my friends think, or even what I think. It's what God thinks that matters to me, because whatever I believe now God will have to address in the Great Day."

> *"And I saw the dead, small and great, stand before God; and the books were opened: and another book was opened, which is the book of life: and the dead were judged out of those things which were written in the books, according to their works."[16]*

> *"Because we have these promises, dear friends, let us cleanse ourselves from everything that can defile our body or spirit. And let us work toward complete holiness because we fear God."[17]*

Judging others without judgmentalism

Just as Jesus knew what was in all men, Holy Ghost knows what is in all men. When you have developed your own consecration He will see that your vision is no longer skewed. He can trust you to judge others. Jesus said:

> *"Do not judge others, and you will not be judged. For you will be treated as you treat others. The standard*

---

[16] Revelation 20:12 KJV.
[17] 2 Corinthians 7:1 NLT.

you use in judging is the standard by which you will be judged.

"And why worry about a speck in your friend's eye when you have a log in your own? How can you think of saying to your friend, 'Let me help you get rid of that speck in your eye,' when you can't see past the log in your own eye? Hypocrite! First get rid of the log in your own eye; then you will see well enough to deal with the speck in your friend's eye."[18]

WHAT THIS MEANS TO YOU

Move into a dimension of holiness where you're expecting God to move in your life even though you may not know what He's going to do next. Open yourself up for God to surprise you. God reveals deep things by His Spirit. Make yourself available so that the Spirit can speak to your spiritual ears. Practice listening to my Friend and "study to be quiet."[19]

"But as it is written, Eye hath not seen, nor ear heard, neither have entered into the heart of man, the things which God hath prepared for them that love him. But God hath revealed them unto us by his Spirit: for the Spirit searcheth all things, yea, the deep things of God."[20]

You can't continue to read the same magazines that you used to read before you were saved and when you didn't have Holy Ghost working inside of you. You can't watch the same movies and TV shows and listen to the same music.

Even the world expects you to be different when you say that you are born again and have given your life to Jesus Christ. They have standards even if they are not born again.

---

[18] Matthew 7:1-5 NLT.
[19] 1 Thessalonians 4:11 KJV.
[20] 1 Corinthians 2:9-10 KJV.

> *"They demonstrate that God's law is written in their hearts, for their own conscience and thoughts either accuse them or tell them they are doing right."[21]*

The Bible says that Gentiles without the law do things that are guided by their own conscience.

> *"For when the Gentiles, who have not the law, do by nature the things contained in the law, these, having not the law, are a law unto themselves: Who show the work of the law written in their hearts, their conscience also bearing witness, and their thoughts the mean while accusing or else excusing one another."[22]*

The Gentiles saw the children of Israel who profaned God's holy name.[23] They probably said, "If you are an example of a child of God I don't want to become one."

Don't let anyone ever say that about you. Consecrate yourself. Perfect your personal holiness and build your relationship with my Friend until everyone can see that you are a genuine child of God most holy.

SEVEN REASONS FOR CONSECRATION

A consecrated person is living proof that Jesus did not give His life in vain. Your holy lifestyle is evidence of the Holy Spirit at work inside of you.

> ***Are you willing to consecrate yourself to the service of the Lord?***

---

[21] Romans 2:15 NLT.
[22] Romans 2:14-15 KJV.
[23] See Ezekiel 36:20.

"Furthermore David the king said unto all the congregation, Solomon my son, whom alone God hath chosen, is yet young and tender, and the work is great: for the palace is not for man, but for the Lord God.

"Now I have prepared with all my might for the house of my God the gold for things to be made of gold, and the silver for things of silver, and the brass for things of brass, the iron for things of iron, and wood for things of wood; onyx stones, and stones to be set, glistering stones, and of divers colours, and all manner of precious stones, and marble stones in abundance.

"Moreover, because I have set my affection to the house of my God, I have of mine own proper good, of gold and silver, which I have given to the house of my God, over and above all that I have prepared for the holy house,

"Even three thousand talents of gold, of the gold of Ophir, and seven thousand talents of refined silver, to overlay the walls of the houses withal:

"The gold for things of gold, and the silver for things of silver, and for all manner of work to be made by the hands of artificers."

"And who then is willing to consecrate his service this day unto the Lord?"[24]

The following list of *Seven Reasons for Consecration*[25] is an excerpt from my book by that name.

(1) Consecration prepares you for an unknown future (Joshua 3:2-17).

(2). Consecration prepares you to stand before two people: God and your enemies (Joshua 7:6-14).

---

[24] 1 Chronicles 29:1-5 KJV.
[25] For further study, I recommend my three-CD series entitled "Consecration" available from Wellington Boone Ministries, www.WellingtonBoone.com.

(3). Consecration purifies your heart motivations. Your consecration represents your purity (Matthew 5:8; Job 1:1, 5).

(4) Consecration averts God's judgment and brings God's presence (Joel 2:15-17; Hebrews 10:26-31).

(5) Consecration makes the spiritually weak strong. Sanctification is your way to perfection and maturity (Hebrews 7:23-28, 10:14).

(6) Consecration is your way to God through the blood of Jesus, who is our High Priest forever—"holy, harmless, undefiled, separate from sinners"— interceding on our behalf (Hebrews 7:17-28; Jeremiah 13:15-17).

(7) Jesus is our role model for a consecrated life (Hebrews 10:9-14; 2 Timothy 2:17-21).

If you want to be spiritually strong, you must enter into a permanent consecration with God. Consecration makes the spiritually weak strong—not just temporarily strong like the Old Testament priests who did temporary service and then died. Jesus your High Priest ever lives to make intercession for you so that you can stay consecrated. He gave you Holy Ghost as your Friend. Everything you need for consecration is available to you now.

13

MY FRIEND'S FRUIT
AND YOUR LIFESTYLE

"For whom he did foreknow, he also did
predestinate to be conformed to the image of
his Son, that he might be the firstborn among
many brethren."[1]

". . . the fruit of the Spirit is love, joy, peace,
longsuffering, gentleness, goodness, faith,
meekness, temperance."[2]

When God created the heavens and the earth and then male and female, notice how many times the Bible says, *"God saw that it was good."[3]* Adam and his wife were good and every one of their children were supposed to be great because God was the explanation for their lives. They came from God!

Without the Fall, no one would have had to encourage you that you are going to have an exceptional life. You were made by God! But when man failed God had to make a covenant promise to send Jesus so we could find Him again through repentance. When you recognize that you have

---

[1] Romans 8:29 KJV.
[2] Galatians 5:22-23 KJV.
[3] Genesis 1:9 and other verses.

rebelled against God and say, "Please forgive me," in that forgiveness you are restored and the sense of an exceptional life returns. You are the glory of God!

God created you to fulfill His destiny. When you are right with God, becoming like Jesus, and filled with the Holy Ghost, you can bring everything on earth into alignment with God. You can become God's champion. God drives out the ugliness in you and you drive out the ugliness in the culture.

God's goal—your transformation

When you are born again, God's incorruptible seed is inside of you. It is part of your new nature. It lives in you. It will not go away. All it needs to do is grow.

> *"Being born again, not of corruptible seed, but of incorruptible, by the word of God, which liveth and abideth for ever."[4]*

> **God's ultimate goal for you isn't right behavior. It is right transformation. Once you are conformed to the image of His Son, God can fix everything else in your life.**

> *"For whom he did foreknow, he also did predestinate to be conformed to the image of his Son, that he might be the firstborn among many brethren."[5]*

After He fixes you, you can fix anything else.

Holy Ghost everywhere at once

Jesus couldn't be everywhere at once because He came in the form of a man, but the Person of the Holy Ghost *is*

---

[4] 1 Peter 1:23 KJV.
[5] Romans 8:29 KJV.

everywhere at once. Holy Ghost is here to give you His personal attention so that you will know how to please God in your character and lifestyle and you can fulfill His will.

God sent Holy Ghost here to produce the certainty that His will can be done at the highest level. He has every confidence that He will get a glorious church.[6] He ordained it. He said it. He wrote it. God has already determined the direction where things are going. Nothing in your life can stop God. Nothing hinders Jesus.

> *"Ride on King Jesus*
> *No man can-a-hinder me*
> *Ride on King Jesus*
> *Ride on*
> *No man can-a-hinder me*
> *No man can-a-hinder me."[7]*

Anyone who stands against you is on the losing side

When you are on God's side, anybody who stands against you has just moved to the losing side. They are destined for defeat. The devil, the world, and evil people all lose if they fight against someone being led by my Friend. You are destined to win. Death, hell, the grave, sickness, sin, and evil demons have all been defeated by Jesus.

THE GOOD FRUIT OF THE SPIRIT—CHARACTER

In some Christian circles, fruit is defined as the number of souls you have won to Christ, how many people got born again in your church, the size of your mailing list, or how many

---

[6] See Ephesians 5:27.
[7] "Ride On, King Jesus." Traditional Negro Spiritual. Lyrics provided by New Life Inspirational Gospel Choir of Atlanta, Georgia. Online at http://www.nligc.org/songs/rideon.html. Accessed November 2011.

showed up in your meetings. In reality, fruit is character. When you bring forth fruit after your kind, it is either the fruit of the flesh or the fruit of my Friend, Holy Ghost.

> *"Therefore be imitators of God, as beloved children; and walk in love, just as Christ also loved you and gave Himself up for us."*[8]

Fruit of the flesh vs. fruit of the Spirit

In the New Testament, Galatians 5 tells you specifically what is meant by Holy Ghost fruit and how it contrasts with the fruit of your sinful nature.

> *"When you follow the desires of your sinful nature, the results are very clear: sexual immorality, impurity, lustful pleasures, idolatry, sorcery, hostility, quarreling, jealousy, outbursts of anger, selfish ambition, dissension, division, envy, drunkenness, wild parties, and other sins like these. Let me tell you again, as I have before, that anyone living that sort of life will not inherit the Kingdom of God.*

> *"But the Holy Spirit produces this kind of fruit in our lives: love, joy, peace, patience, kindness, goodness, faithfulness, gentleness, and self-control. There is no law against these things!"*[9]

Character grown from the inside out—inner attributes

Because of Greco-Roman influence and the American external mindset, a discussion of better character always moves to something external—some standards of behavior that are imposed outwardly.

---

[8] Ephesians 5:1-2 NASB.
[9] Galatians 5:19-23 NLT.

Modern methods focus on training and discipline. However, the Bible places the focus on a supernatural work on the inside and what my Friend is doing *in you*, because when He gets the inside right, the outside happens.

When God made man in His image, He gave us inner attributes so that we could look like Him. God is a Spirit and He made man a spiritual being. He made Adam, and ultimately He made you, so that you would think like Him, speak like Him, carry His nature, and bear Holy Ghost fruit—love, joy, peace, longsuffering or patience, gentleness, goodness, faith, meekness, and temperance or self-control.

Some of my Black brethren are discovering that because of the geographic location where Adam was created that potentially Adam was a man of dark complexion or what we would call a Black man. Actually, what is a Black man? Are we referring to the color of the skin? Or are we referring to a race? What is a White man?

Forget about being defined by your skin. You need to be defined by your godly character, which is the fruit of the Holy Ghost within you. When God says He created man after His likeness, that has nothing to do with how Adam looked physically. God's image and likeness are inner attributes.

MAN'S CHARACTER IN THE IMAGE OF GOD

Adam was given three abilities that made him like God. He possessed the ability to choose, the ability to reason, and the image or character of God.

When you get saved, the Lord doesn't make you conform to Jesus' external appearance. If He did, all of us would probably have to get a different shade of skin tone and hair and everything else so you could tell us apart.

God conforms the church to the inner qualities of Christ-likeness. If you look at history since the Fall, the greatest place where we have missed God is in the area of character, in the inward realm. The way we see inwardly and the way we believe in the inner realm of our thinking determines what we do and how we act.

You don't exist by chance but for God's purposes

God is the reason that you exist, not chance. If you believe you are a product of evolution, you are wandering in circles. You think you are the result of some cosmic accident instead of realizing that God specifically created you in His image and He made you to bear fruit after His kind.

The story of Adam in Genesis is true. God had a creative purpose when He made Adam and He had a creative purpose when He made you. Before you understand what God wants you to do, you have to understand who He created you to be, because being always precedes doing. That is why you need to know a Friend Who is God. You need to ask why God created you and you need to adhere to what He tells you to do.

It was the Lord who decided, "Let us make man." God made us in His image. He is the Divine Potter and we are clay in His hands. We owe Him our absolute allegiance.. Even though we are fallen, He sees us not as we are but as He ordained us to be.

Purifying your conscience to represent God

Paul wrote to the church in Corinth about sin in their lives that affected their access before God and kept them walking in guilt. Their consciences were not consecrated. They didn't feel good about themselves. They were not letting the Lord get next to them.

It's amazing that before any man ever rebukes you the Holy Ghost is already there dealing with you from within. When you allow your conscience to be purified, you can trust your conscience. When you become sincere and stop "putting on," you can trust the inner witness of your spirit.

Part of the reason you don't know how to walk in the Spirit is that you don't allow God to deal with your conscience, your inner self. You don't let Him into the shadows so you don't have confidence that it's God's voice. You keep thinking, "Should I do this or should I do that?" because the shadows are still there. Paul gave us an example of how he conducted himself within. He talked about a circumstance where he had to depend totally upon God.

> *"But we had the sentence of death in ourselves, that we should not trust in ourselves, but in God which raiseth the dead."[10]*

Paul was saying that God can raise the dead and he was also talking about consecration as a type of being raised from the dead. You are dead in sin and God raises you from the dead. You can walk in such favor with God that you believe there is nothing that you cannot accomplish—not by trying to muster up faith but by submitting to the purifying of the Lord on the altars of total dedication and receiving faith. You can rise up from those altars comforted that God is not only answering prayers but you are the answer of God for the things you are praying for.

We have been living too long at the level of existence. We are praying for God to give us something. We are praying for something material so we can raise our level—more money, more things—but we don't realize that we are here as God's answer to somebody else's need here on the earth.

Paul was in prison many times. He was beaten. Many times he faced death. He was in deep water. In 2 Corinthians 11 he gives us his testimony. He was in perils. Many times he was beaten. He was under the sentence of death—literally, physically, almost brought to the place of death.

However, because my Friend was there with him, those experiences renewed his trust in God. The actual circumstances were doing nothing but strengthening him to depend on God more. And it proved that the first commitment he made to God on the altar was a serious commitment. His circumstances were proving to himself, his own conscience, that he was a serious

---

[10] 2 Corinthians 1:9 KJV.

191

Christian. Paul did not try to avoid circumstances. He went through them because of his dedication. He became more pure and walked with a new holiness and took more ground.

WHAT THIS MEANS TO YOU

Your conscience is an aspect of your spirit. When Holy Ghost is your Friend, your conscience tells you that you have conducted yourself the way God would conduct Himself. Your wisdom comes from God and you have the mind of Christ.

> *"But as it is written, Eye hath not seen, nor ear heard, neither have entered into the heart of man, the things which God hath prepared for them that love him.*
>
> *"But God hath revealed them unto us by his Spirit: for the Spirit searcheth all things, yea, the deep things of God. For what man knoweth the things of a man, save the spirit of man which is in him? even so the things of God knoweth no man, but the Spirit of God. Now we have received, not the spirit of the world, but the spirit which is of God; that we might know the things that are freely given to us of God. Which things also we speak, not in the words which man's wisdom teacheth, but which the Holy Ghost teacheth; comparing spiritual things with spiritual.*
>
> *"But the natural man receiveth not the things of the Spirit of God: for they are foolishness unto him: neither can he know them, because they are spiritually discerned. But he that is spiritual judgeth all things, yet he himself is judged of no man. For who hath known the mind of the Lord, that he may instruct him? But we have the mind of Christ."*[11]

In what ways can you see that God is good and He has given you the mind of Christ and the fruit of the Spirit?

---

[11] 1 Corinthians 2:9-16 KJV.

14

MAKING HOLY GHOST
YOUR BEST FRIEND

"Ointment and perfume rejoice the heart:
so doth the sweetness of a man's friend
by hearty counsel."[1]

L et's say a husband and wife decide to go on a vacation together. They are sharing the same hotel room but for the whole day they never even acknowledge that the other person is there. What would that be like? Would the other person feel valued? Is that any way to treat Holy Ghost?

You don't have to take a special trip to get alone with my Friend. Jesus said the Holy Ghost will abide with you forever. He's been with you the whole day. Have you acknowledged Him? If not, that means you don't value what He brings with Him. He could drive out your discomfort about life if you would let Him in. He could totally resolve the issues that concern you. The first place to start is to acknowledge Him and make Him your Best Friend.

How Someone Becomes a Best Friend

Someone becomes your best friend when you favor

---

[1] Proverbs 27:9 KJV.

him. You're the one he can always turn to. You're the one who really cares. You listen to him. You would sacrifice everything for him. You would lay down your lives for one another.

> *"Greater love has no man than this that a man would lay down his life for his friend."[2]*

When you hear a friend talking you don't even have to see him to know it's him. You know how his voice sounds, you know his tone, you can tell by his disposition. Do you know Holy Ghost that way?

Friends can correct you when you're wrong

Jesus said, "I'm going to send you *another* Comforter."
What do friends do for one another? They comfort you. Jesus was saying, "I am a Comforter and so is He."
Friends sometimes comfort you by correcting you. How can a friend correct you if you don't let him in? You know Somebody Who really wants to look out for you but you say, "No, no, that's all right. I don't need You. Please don't talk to me. I don't want to hear it."
Have we actually said to Holy Ghost, "I don't want to hear what You are saying"?
A friend doesn't always tell you what you want to hear. If he is a good friend he tells you what you *need* to hear. That's also what makes him a friend because he is not just a seasonal friend. A real friend will look you right in your face and tell you that you're wrong.
I love to hear about a husband and wife who can be honest with one another. A man told me, "Say, look, I can't bowl with you tonight. I've got to go home and spend the evening with my wife." Maybe she had corrected him because he wasn't coming home enough. Would you respond in love to your wife if she wanted you home more often or is there a potential that you may be married to a woman but you are not

---

[2] Footnote

friends with her? You have a marriage covenant but you have not consummated it with your actions?

How many times has Holy Ghost told you "No!" and you listened? He said, "No. I don't want you to go there and do that with those other people. I want you to do something with Me." If He said that, would you listen?

I was with a man who said, "Look, guys, I have to leave so I can go home and cook dinner for my wife." I can't remember the last time somebody said that to me. Tell me if that doesn't endear a husband to his wife when he cooks so she doesn't have to cook all the time! I was so happy to hear that somebody thought that way. That man was saying just because his wife is a woman that doesn't mean she has to do all the cooking. That can create a sacrificial friendship, the same kind you need to cultivate with my Friend.

Friends are comfortable hanging out together

A real friend always wants you around.

Some people who are married don't want to be around one another because they have never cultivated friendship. You can be married and promise to be with your wife forever but you still haven't learned how to hang out with her—just to listen to her talk. Maybe she isn't talking about anything that's world-changing. She's just talking but you know that it may be one of those times when she just needs to know if anybody wants to listen to her. That's what a friend does.

If you are a wife, you need to be careful because you may not call your husband a servant but the way you treat him indicates that you think of him that way. You may treat your husband like a slave because all you talk about is how he needs to be a better provider. You say you can't wait until he makes more money so you can quit work. I have heard women say that. You can't be as old as I am and not have heard that.

Is Holy Ghost your Friend only when your needs are met? Do you turn Him off when your money runs out?

Or do you recognize that you have a covenant with a Real Friend and your best days lie ahead?

GETTING IN POSITION TO RULE AND REIGN IN ETERNITY

When you remember the greatness of God you will appreciate the power He has that He might share with you if you are His Best Friend.

> *"'To whom will you compare me?*
>> *Who is my equal?' asks the Holy One.*
>
> *"Look up into the heavens.*
>> *Who created all the stars?*
> *He brings them out like an army, one after another,*
>> *calling each by its name.*
> *Because of his great power and incomparable strength,*
>> *not a single one is missing.*
> *O Jacob, how can you say the LORD does not see your troubles?*
>> *O Israel, how can you say God ignores your rights?*
> *Have you never heard?*
>> *Have you never understood?*
> *The LORD is the everlasting God,*
>> *the Creator of all the earth.*
> *He never grows weak or weary.[3]*
>> *No one can measure the depths of his understanding.*
> *He gives power to the weak*
>> *and strength to the powerless.*
> *Even youths will become weak and tired,*
>> *and young men will fall in exhaustion.*
> *But those who trust in the Lord will find new strength.*
>> *They will soar high on wings like eagles.*
> *They will run and not grow weary.*
>> *They will walk and not faint."*

God measures the heavens by the span of His hand. There is nothing He doesn't understand. When you talk to God,

---

[3] Isaiah 40:25-31 NLT.

turn everything not just into a prayer but also into a discussion you would have with your Best Friend.

Holy Ghost wants to use somebody who is willing to show that God is alive. He can show up mystically. He can show up in the atmosphere and the atmosphere is charged.

However, Jesus gets the most credit on earth when He shows up inside a Christian. You must be the person He shows up in. Your church should grow just on the basis of the impact you have on people's lives as Your Friend leads you every day.

Trusting you to rule over worlds

God gave worldwide dominion to Adam but Adam failed the test and lost his authority. God is preparing you to become like the Last Adam, Jesus, so that He can entrust you to rule over worlds.

This life is just a seed life. You are being positioned to rule and reign with Christ. God cast the devil out of heaven so He certainly doesn't want us to take the devil back there by acting like snakes. He wants us to learn how to become a worm. God is using your circumstances on earth to get the snake out of you now so that He can use you in the future to rule in eternity.

Worms do not strike back like snakes. Even when stepped on, they are easily crushed. The Holy Spirit's nature is a gentle nature like a worm. He doesn't promote Himself. He promotes Jesus. He is kind—even when He takes strong actions against evil. He is pure and holy. He never leads you astray but only leads you into the truth.

You are the hope of creation

All of creation is depending on you to follow the proper Guide. Ever since Adam, Christians have been the hope of creation.

"For the earnest expectation of the creature waiteth for the manifestation of the sons of God."[4]

What the first Adam lost, the Last Adam, Christ, restored. You are more than a conqueror in Christ. You can have an impact that is impossible for you to measure.

"If God be for us, who can be against us? He that spared not his own Son, but delivered him up for us all, how shall he not with him also freely give us all things? Who shall lay any thing to the charge of God's elect? It is God that justifieth. Who is he that condemneth? It is Christ that died, yea rather, that is risen again, who is even at the right hand of God, who also maketh intercession for us. Who shall separate us from the love of Christ? shall tribulation, or distress, or persecution, or famine, or nakedness, or peril, or sword?

"As it is written, For thy sake we are killed all the day long; we are accounted as sheep for the slaughter.

"Nay, in all these things we are more than conquerors through him that loved us."[5]

You can bring restoration by your consecration and your Friendship with Holy Ghost. God's abundant life through Jesus Christ can be yours, and abundant life can be restored to earth—through you.

RISING UP WITH YOUR BEST FRIEND

It is your time to rise up now. You cannot be bought by money. You were already bought by the blood of Jesus. You have too much Holy Ghost in you to be limited by your gender,

---

[4] Romans 8:19 KJV.
[5] Romans 8:31-37 KJV.

your race, your economic status, or your lack of education or influence.

Two steps you can take

1. Set a specific time to meet with your Friend every day. Tell Him, "This is my time between You and me." Don't start with a commitment you can't keep. Choose something where you know you can be faithful and then move toward spending more time together.

2. Ask Holy Ghost to help you to do something you have never done. This will be your adventure into the dimension where He lives.

Some day you will walk into the next world together

Jesus said that we would receive power from Holy Ghost to be His witnesses, both in Judea, and Samaria, and to the uttermost parts of the earth.[6] You can be an example in your home, city, and the uttermost parts of the world and then walk right on out into eternity, just like Enoch.

The Bible says that Enoch pleased God and he never died. He was just gone.

"And Enoch walked with God: and he was not; for God took him."[7]

You should have so much Holy Ghost and be so much like God that you can walk right out of this life into the next life without dying or even having to change. You walk in the Holy Spirit life here as you will walk like God there.

---

[6] See Acts 1:8.
[7] Genesis 5:24 KJV.

When you have no more use for this world, God can say to you, "Come on and walk with Me on into this next world. You don't even need to see death."

And then you and your Friend will walk right out into eternity together and you will see Jesus face to face.

APPENDICES

APPENDIX 1

PLACES WHERE MY FRIEND
SHOWS UP IN THE BIBLE
He Is Awesome Wherever He Goes![1]

Throughout this book I have noted many crucial places where Holy Ghost was there. He is everywhere throughout the Bible, but certain places need to be highlighted so He will not be missed or ignored. He was there at creation. He was active in every aspect of Jesus' life—conception, baptism, anointing and public call to ministry, led Jesus into the wilderness to be tempted by the devil, raised Jesus from the dead, came to the disciples at Pentecost with the Baptism in the Holy Ghost (the promise of the Father). The acts of the apostles are the acts of the Holy Ghost

My Friend was there throughout the Old Testament and with the patriarchs and major and minor prophets. As He revealed the reality of God's will to them, their ability became more about what God was about than what they were about. Their priorities, their destiny, and the way they lived their lives pointed to God as the explanation. The Bible gives us a warning:

> *"These things happened to them as examples for us. They were written down to warn us who live at the end of the age."*[2]

All of Scripture is a model for us. It is God's interaction with people through the power of the Holy Spirit. God took care of the ordination. Jesus took care of the administration and Holy Ghost took care of the manifestation. All three members of the Godhead were involved. They are One God with different responsibilities.

---

[1] Highlights call attention to certain parts of each passage but you may see other parts or other passages that are also significant. Some passages were omitted if it was not clear if they referred to Holy Ghost. Most Scripture verses are from the King James Version with other translations noted, if added.

[2] 1 Corinthians 10:11 NLT.

---

4 Questions to Ask When You Find Holy Ghost in the Bible

Ask these questions as you read about our Friend:

1.   Where is He found in Scripture?
2.   What is He doing there?
3.   What is the result of His being there?
4.   What does it mean to us today?

KING JAMES TRANSLATION—USAGE OF THE WORDS "HOLY GHOST"

When the King James Version of the Bible was published in 1611, the New Testament translators used the name "Holy Ghost" many more times than they used "Holy Spirit" to translate the same Greek words for the Third Person of the Godhead—*pneuma hagion.*

The word *pneuma* is from the Greek verb *pneo,* meaning "to breathe" or "to blow."

The word *hagion* means "holy."

Jesus demonstrated the association between the word "to breathe" and the coming of the Holy Ghost when He breathed on His disciples and said, "Receive the Holy Ghost."

> *"And when [Jesus] had said this, he breathed on them, and saith unto them, Receive ye the Holy Ghost."*[3]

Holy Ghost is the breath of God Who blows wherever He wills. Jesus said to Nicodemus:

> " *'You must be born again.' The wind blows wherever it wants. Just as you can hear the wind but can't tell where it comes from or where it is going, so you can't explain how people are born of the Spirit.'"*[4]

More recent translations of the Bible don't use the words "Holy Ghost" because of a change in the meaning of words since those days. Today we usually think of a ghost as a demonic, cloudlike apparition that looks like a dead man. However, in 1611, "Ghost" meant someone who had the same *essence* as the person who had departed. Holy Ghost had the same *essence* as the Person of Jesus, Who had departed to be with His Father!

---

[3] John 20:22 KJV.
[4] John 3:7-8 NLT.

Regardless of the words that are used by a translator, however, our focus is the Holy Ghost as the Third Person of the Godhead—Father, Son, and Holy Ghost. They are coequal and by some mystery known only to God They are Three in One. Our God is One.

I have chosen to use "Holy Ghost" as the title of this book to draw attention to our oft-neglected Friend.

SELECTED INCIDENCES OF HOLY GHOST IN OLD AND NEW TESTAMENTS

272 Selected Passages (some include more than one verse)
79 passages from the Old Testament
193 passages from the New Testament

OLD TESTAMENT SCRIPTURES

1.	Genesis 1:2. And the earth was without form, and void; and darkness was upon the face of the deep. And the Spirit of God moved upon the face of the waters.
2.	Genesis 6:3. And the LORD[5] said, My spirit shall not always strive with man, for that he also is flesh: yet his days shall be an hundred and twenty years.
3.	Genesis 41:38. And Pharaoh said unto his servants, Can we find such a one as this is, a man in whom the Spirit of God is?
4.	Exodus 31:3. And I have filled him with the spirit of God, in wisdom, and in understanding, and in knowledge, and in all manner of workmanship.
5.	Exodus 35:31. And he hath filled him with the spirit of God, in wisdom, in understanding, and in knowledge, and in all manner of workmanship.
6.	Numbers 11:29. And Moses said unto him, Enviest thou for my sake? would God that all the LORD's people were prophets, and that the LORD would put his spirit upon them!
7.	Numbers 24:2. And Balaam lifted up his eyes, and he saw Israel abiding in his tents according to their tribes; and the spirit of God came upon him.
8.	Numbers 27:18. And the LORD said unto Moses, Take thee Joshua the son of Nun, a man in whom is the spirit, and lay thine hand upon him.
9.	Judges 3:10. And the Spirit of the LORD came upon him, and he judged Israel, and went out to war: and the LORD delivered Chushan-rishathaim king of Mesopotamia into his hand; and his hand prevailed against Chushan-rishathaim.

---

[5] "LORD" in small caps refers to the Hebrew word YHWH.

10.	Judges 6:34. But the Spirit of the LORD came upon Gideon, and he blew a trumpet; and Abi-ezer was gathered after him.
11.	Judges 11:29. Then the Spirit of the LORD came upon Jephthah, and he passed over Gilead, and Manasseh, and passed over Mizpeh of Gilead, and from Mizpeh of Gilead he passed over unto the children of Ammon.
12.	Judges 13:25. And the Spirit of the LORD began to move him at times in the camp of Dan between Zorah and Eshtaol.
13.	Judges 14:6. And the Spirit of the LORD came mightily upon him, and he rent him as he would have rent a kid, and he had nothing in his hand: but he told not his father or his mother what he had done.
14.	Judges 14:19. And the Spirit of the LORD came upon him, and he went down to Ashkelon, and slew thirty men of them, and took their spoil, and gave change of garments unto them which expounded the riddle. And his anger was kindled, and he went up to his father's house.
15.	Judges 15:14. And when he came unto Lehi, the Philistines shouted against him: and the Spirit of the LORD came mightily upon him, and the cords that were upon his arms became as flax that was burnt with fire, and his bands loosed from off his hands.
16.	1 Samuel 10:6. And the Spirit of the LORD will come upon thee, and thou shalt prophesy with them, and shalt be turned into another man.
17.	1 Samuel 10:10. And when they came thither to the hill, behold, a company of prophets met him; and the Spirit of God came upon him, and he prophesied among them.
18.	1 Samuel 11:6. And the Spirit of God came upon Saul when he heard those tidings, and his anger was kindled greatly.
19.	1 Samuel 16:13-14. Then Samuel took the horn of oil, and anointed him in the midst of his brethren: and the Spirit of the LORD came upon David from that day forward. So Samuel rose up, and went to Ramah. But the Spirit of the LORD departed from Saul, and an evil spirit from the LORD troubled him.
20.	1 Samuel 19:20. And Saul sent messengers to take David: and when they saw the company of the prophets prophesying, and Samuel standing as appointed over them, the Spirit of God was upon the messengers of Saul, and they also prophesied.
21.	1 Samuel 19:23. And he went thither to Naioth in Ramah: and the Spirit of God was upon him also, and he went on, and prophesied, until he came to Naioth in Ramah.
22.	2 Samuel 23:2. The Spirit of the LORD spake by me, and his word was in my tongue.
23.	1 Kings 18:12. And it shall come to pass, as soon as I am gone from thee, that the Spirit of the LORD shall carry thee whither I know not; and so when I come and tell Ahab, and he cannot find thee, he shall slay me: but I thy servant fear the LORD from my youth.

24. 1 Kings 22:24. But Zedekiah the son of Chenaanah went near, and smote Micaiah on the cheek, and said, Which way went the Spirit of the LORD from me to speak unto thee?

25. 2 Kings 2:16. And they said unto him, Behold now, there be with thy servants fifty strong men; let them go, we pray thee, and seek thy master: lest peradventure the Spirit of the LORD hath taken him up, and cast him upon some mountain, or into some valley. And he said, Ye shall not send.

26. 2 Chronicles 15:1. And the Spirit of God came upon Azariah the son of Oded.

27. 2 Chronicles 18:23. Then Zedekiah the son of Chenaanah came near, and smote Micaiah upon the cheek, and said, Which way went the Spirit of the LORD from me to speak unto thee?

28. 2 Chronicles 20:14. Then upon Jahaziel the son of Zechariah, the son of Benaiah, the son of Jeiel, the son of Mattaniah, a Levite of the sons of Asaph came the Spirit of the LORD in the midst of the congregation.

29. 2 Chronicles 24:20. And the Spirit of God came upon Zechariah the son of Jehoiada the priest, which stood above the people, and said unto them, Thus saith God, Why transgress ye the commandments of the LORD, that ye cannot prosper? because ye have forsaken the LORD, he hath also forsaken you.

30. Nehemiah 9:20. Thou gavest also thy good spirit to instruct them, and withheldest not thy manna from their mouth, and gavest them water for their thirst.

31. Nehemiah 9:30. Yet many years didst thou forbear them, and testifiedst against them by thy spirit in thy prophets: yet would they not give ear: therefore gavest thou them into the hand of the people of the lands.

32. Job 26:13. By his spirit he hath garnished the heavens; his hand hath formed the crooked serpent.

33. Job 27:3. All the while my breath is in me, and the spirit of God is in my nostrils.

34. Job 32:8. But there is a spirit in man: and the inspiration of the Almighty giveth them understanding.

35. Job 33:4. The Spirit of God hath made me, and the breath of the Almighty hath given me life.

36. Job 34:14. If he set his heart upon man, if he gather unto himself his spirit and his breath.

37. Psalms 51:11. Cast me not away from thy presence; and take not thy holy spirit from me.

38. Psalms 51:12. Restore unto me the joy of thy salvation; and uphold me with thy free spirit.

39. Psalms 104:30. Thou sendest forth thy spirit, they are created: and thou renewest the face of the earth.

40. Psalms 139:7. Whither shall I go from thy spirit? or whither shall I flee from thy presence?

41.	Psalms 143:10. Teach me to do thy will; for thou art my God: thy spirit is good; lead me into the land of uprightness.
42.	Proverbs 1:23. Turn you at my reproof: behold I will pour out my spirit unto you, I will make known my words unto you.
43.	Ecclesiastes 11:5. As thou knowest not what is the way of the spirit, nor how the bones do grow in the womb of her that is with child: even so thou knowest not the works of God who maketh all.
44.	Ecclesiastes 12:7. Then shall the dust return to the earth as it was: and the spirit shall return unto God who gave it.
45.	Isaiah 11:2. And the spirit of the LORD shall rest upon him, the spirit of wisdom and understanding, the spirit of counsel and might, the spirit of knowledge and of the fear of the LORD;
46.	Isaiah 30:1. Woe to the rebellious children, saith the LORD, that take counsel, but not of me; and that cover with a covering, but not of my spirit, that they may add sin to sin.
47.	Isaiah 32:15. Until the spirit be poured upon us from on high, and the wilderness be a fruitful field, and the fruitful field be counted for a forest.
48.	Isaiah 34:16. Seek ye out of the book of the LORD, and read: no one of these shall fail, none shall want her mate: for my mouth it hath commanded, and his spirit it hath gathered them.
49.	Isaiah 40:7. The grass withereth, the flower fadeth: because the spirit of the LORD bloweth upon it: surely the people is grass.
50.	Isaiah 40:13. Who hath directed the Spirit of the LORD, or being his counseller hath taught him?
51.	Isaiah 42:1. Behold my servant, whom I uphold; mine elect, in whom my soul delighteth; I have put my spirit upon him: he shall bring forth judgment to the Gentiles.
52.	Isaiah 44:3. For I will pour water upon him that is thirsty, and floods upon the dry ground: I will pour my spirit upon thy seed, and my blessing upon thine offspring.
53.	Isaiah 48:16. Come ye near unto me, hear ye this; I have not spoken in secret from the beginning; from the time that it was, there am I: and now the Lord GOD, and his Spirit, hath sent me.
54.	Isaiah 59:19. So shall they fear the name of the LORD from the west, and his glory from the rising of the sun. When the enemy shall come in like a flood, the Spirit of the LORD shall lift up a standard against him.
55.	Isaiah 59:21. As for me, this is my covenant with them, saith the LORD; My spirit that is upon thee, and my words which I have put in thy mouth, shall not depart out of thy mouth, nor out of the mouth of thy seed, nor out of the mouth of thy seed's seed, saith the LORD, from henceforth and for ever.
56.	Isaiah 61:1. The Spirit of the Lord GOD is upon me; because the LORD hath anointed me to preach good tidings unto the meek; he hath sent me to bind up the brokenhearted, to proclaim liberty to the captives, and the opening of the prison to them that are bound.

57. Isaiah 63:10. But they rebelled, and vexed his holy Spirit: therefore he was turned to be their enemy, and he fought against them.

58. Isaiah 63:11. Then he remembered the days of old, Moses, and his people, saying, Where is he that brought them up out of the sea with the shepherd of his flock? where is he that put his holy Spirit within him?

59. Isaiah 63:14. As a beast goeth down into the valley, the Spirit of the LORD caused him to rest: so didst thou lead thy people, to make thyself a glorious name.

60. Ezekiel 2:2. And the spirit entered into me when he spake unto me, and set me upon my feet, that I heard him that spake unto me.

61. Ezekiel 3:12. Then the spirit took me up, and I heard behind me a voice of a great rushing, saying, Blessed be the glory of the LORD from his place.

62. Ezekiel 3:14. So the spirit lifted me up, and took me away, and I went in bitterness, in the heat of my spirit; but the hand of the LORD was strong upon me.

63. Ezekiel 3:24. Then the spirit entered into me, and set me upon my feet, and spake with me, and said unto me, Go, shut thyself within thine house.

64. Ezekiel 8:3. And he put forth the form of an hand, and took me by a lock of mine head; and the spirit lifted me up between the earth and the heaven, and brought me in the visions of God to Jerusalem, to the door of the inner gate that looketh toward the north; where was the seat of the image of jealousy, which provoketh to jealousy.

65. Ezekiel 11:1. Moreover the spirit lifted me up, and brought me unto the east gate of the LORD's house, which looketh eastward: and behold at the door of the gate five and twenty men; among whom I saw Jaazaniah the son of Azur, and Pelatiah the son of Benaiah, the princes of the people.

66. Ezekiel 11:5. And the Spirit of the LORD fell upon me, and said unto me, Speak; Thus saith the LORD; Thus have ye said, O house of Israel: for I know the things that come into your mind, every one of them.

67. Ezekiel 11:24. Afterwards the spirit took me up, and brought me in a vision by the Spirit of God into Chaldea, to them of the captivity. So the vision that I had seen went up from me.

68. Ezekiel 36:27. And I will put my spirit within you, and cause you to walk in my statutes, and ye shall keep my judgments, and do them.

69. Ezekiel 37:1. The hand of the LORD was upon me and carried me out in the spirit of the LORD, and set me down in the midst of the valley which was full of bones.

70. Ezekiel 37:14. And shall put my spirit in you, and ye shall live, and I shall place you in your own land: then shall ye know that I the LORD have spoken it, and performed it, saith the LORD.

71. Ezekiel 39:29. Neither will I hide my face any more from them: for I have poured out my spirit upon the house of Israel, saith the Lord GOD.

72. Ezekiel 43:5. So the spirit took me up, and brought me into the inner court; and, behold, the glory of the LORD filled the house.

73. Joel 2:28-29. And it shall come to pass afterward, that I will pour out my spirit upon all flesh: and your sons and your daughters shall prophesy, your old men shall dream dreams, your young men shall see visions: And also upon the servants and upon the handmaids in those days will I pour out my spirit.

74. Micah 2:7. O thou that art named the house of Jacob, is the spirit of the LORD straitened? are these his doings? do not my words do good to him that walketh uprightly?
NLT. Should you talk that way, O family of Israel?
Will the Lord's Spirit have patience with such behavior?
If you would do what is right,
you would find my words comforting.

75. Micah 3:8. But truly I am full of power by the spirit of the LORD, and of judgment, and of might, to declare unto Jacob his transgression, and to Israel his sin.

76. Haggai 2:5. According to the word that I covenanted with you when ye came out of Egypt, so my spirit remaineth among you: fear ye not.

77. Zechariah 4:6. Then he answered and spake unto me, saying, This is the word of the LORD unto Zerubbabel, saying, Not by might, nor by power, but by my spirit, saith the LORD of hosts.

78. Zechariah 7:12. Yea, they made their hearts as an adamant stone, lest they should hear the law, and the words which the LORD of hosts hath sent in his spirit by the former prophets: therefore came a great wrath from the LORD of hosts.

79. Malachi 2:14-15. Yet ye say, Wherefore? Because the LORD hath been witness between thee and the wife of thy youth, against whom thou hast dealt treacherously: yet is she thy companion, and the wife of thy covenant. And did not he make one? Yet had he the residue of the spirit. And wherefore one? That he might seek a godly seed. Therefore take heed to your spirit, and let none deal treacherously against the wife of his youth.
NASB. "Yet you say, 'For what reason?' Because the LORD has been a witness between you and the wife of your youth, against whom you have dealt treacherously, though she is your companion and your wife by covenant.
"But not one has done so who has a remnant of the Spirit. And what did that one do while he was seeking a godly offspring? Take heed then to your spirit, and let no one deal treacherously against the wife of your youth."

80.	Matthew 1:18. Now the birth of Jesus Christ was on this wise: When as his mother Mary was espoused to Joseph, before they came together, she was found with child of the Holy Ghost.
81.	Matthew 1:20. But while he thought on these things, behold, the angel of the Lord appeared unto him in a dream, saying, Joseph, thou son of David, fear not to take unto thee Mary thy wife: for that which is conceived in her is of the Holy Ghost.
82.	Matthew 3:11. I indeed baptize you with water unto repentance: but he that cometh after me is mightier than I, whose shoes I am not worthy to bear: he shall baptize you with the Holy Ghost, and with fire.
83.	Matthew 3:16. And Jesus, when he was baptized, went up straightway out of the water: and, lo, the heavens were opened unto him, and he saw the Spirit of God descending like a dove, and lighting upon him.
84.	Matthew 4:1. Then was Jesus led up of the Spirit into the wilderness to be tempted of the devil.
85.	Matthew 12:31-32. Wherefore I say unto you, All manner of sin and blasphemy shall be forgiven unto men: but the blasphemy against the Holy Ghost shall not be forgiven unto men. And whosoever speaketh a word against the Son of man, it shall be forgiven him: but whosoever speaketh against the Holy Ghost, it shall not be forgiven him, neither in this world, neither in the world to come.
86.	Matthew 12:18. Behold my servant, whom I have chosen; my beloved, in whom my soul is well pleased: I will put my spirit upon him, and he shall shew judgment to the Gentiles.
87.	Matthew 12:28. But if I cast out devils by the Spirit of God, then the kingdom of God is come unto you.
88.	Matthew 28:19. Go ye therefore, and teach all nations, baptizing them in the name of the Father, and of the Son, and of the Holy Ghost.
89.	Mark 1:8. I indeed have baptized you with water: but he shall baptize you with the Holy Ghost.
90.	Mark 1:10. And straightway coming up out of the water, he saw the heavens opened, and the Spirit like a dove descending upon him.
91.	Mark 1:12. And immediately the Spirit driveth him into the wilderness.
92.	Mark 3:29. But he that shall blaspheme against the Holy Ghost hath never forgiveness, but is in danger of eternal damnation.
93.	Mark 12:36. For David himself said by the Holy Ghost, The Lord said to my Lord, Sit thou on my right hand, till I make thine enemies thy footstool.

94. Mark 13:11. But when they shall lead you, and deliver you up, take no thought beforehand what ye shall speak, neither do ye premeditate: but whatsoever shall be given you in that hour, that speak ye: for it is not ye that speak, but the Holy Ghost.

95. Luke 1:15. For he shall be great in the sight of the Lord, and shall drink neither wine nor strong drink; and he shall be filled with the Holy Ghost, even from his mother's womb.

96. Luke 1:35. And the angel answered and said unto her, The Holy Ghost shall come upon thee, and the power of the Highest shall overshadow thee: therefore also that holy thing which shall be born of thee shall be called the Son of God.

97. Luke 1:41. And it came to pass, that, when Elisabeth heard the salutation of Mary, the babe leaped in her womb; and Elisabeth was filled with the Holy Ghost.

98. Luke 1:67. And his father Zacharias was filled with the Holy Ghost, and prophesied.

99. Luke 2:25-27. And, behold, there was a man in Jerusalem, whose name was Simeon; and the same man was just and devout, waiting for the consolation of Israel: and the Holy Ghost was upon him. And it was revealed unto him by the Holy Ghost, that he should not see death, before he had seen the Lord's Christ. And he came by the Spirit into the temple: and when the parents brought in the child Jesus, to do for him after the custom of the law.

100. Luke 3:16. John answered, saying unto them all, I indeed baptize you with water; but one mightier than I cometh, the latchet of whose shoes I am not worthy to unloose: he shall baptize you with the Holy Ghost and with fire.

101. Luke 3:22. And the Holy Ghost descended in a bodily shape like a dove upon him, and a voice came from heaven, which said, Thou art my beloved Son; in thee I am well pleased.

102. Luke 4:1. And Jesus being full of the Holy Ghost returned from Jordan, and was led by the Spirit into the wilderness.

103. Luke 4:14. And Jesus returned in the power of the Spirit into Galilee: and there went out a fame of him through all the region round about.

104. Luke 4:18-19. The Spirit of the Lord is upon me, because he hath anointed me to preach the gospel to the poor; he hath sent me to heal the brokenhearted, to preach deliverance to the captives, and recovering of sight to the blind, to set at liberty them that are bruised, To preach the acceptable year of the Lord.

105. Luke 11:13. If ye then, being evil, know how to give good gifts unto your children: how much more shall your heavenly Father give the Holy Spirit to them that ask him?

106. Luke 12:10. And whosoever shall speak a word against the Son of man, it shall be forgiven him: but unto him that blasphemeth against the Holy Ghost it shall not be forgiven.

107. Luke 12:12. For the Holy Ghost shall teach you in the same hour what ye ought to say.

108. John 1:32-33. And John bare record, saying, I saw the Spirit descending from heaven like a dove, and it abode upon him. And I knew him not: but he that sent me to baptize with water, the same said unto me, Upon whom thou shalt see the Spirit descending, and remaining on him, the same is he which baptizeth with the Holy Ghost.

109. John 3:5-6, Jesus answered, Verily, verily, I say unto thee, Except a man be born of water and of the Spirit, he cannot enter into the kingdom of God. That which is born of the flesh is flesh; and that which is born of the Spirit is spirit.

110. John 3:8. The wind bloweth where it listeth, and thou hearest the sound thereof, but canst not tell whence it cometh, and whither it goeth: so is every one that is born of the Spirit.

111. John 3:34. For he whom God hath sent speaketh the words of God: for God giveth not the Spirit by measure unto him.

112. John 4:23-24. But the hour cometh, and now is, when the true worshippers shall worship the Father in spirit and in truth: for the Father seeketh such to worship him. God is a Spirit: and they that worship him must worship him in spirit and in truth.

113. John 6:63. It is the spirit that quickeneth: the flesh profiteth nothing: the words that I speak unto you, they are spirit, and they are life. NLT. The Spirit alone gives eternal life. Human effort accomplishes nothing. And the very words I have spoken to you are spirit and life.

114. John 7:39. But this spake he of the Spirit, which they that believe on him should receive: for the Holy Ghost was not yet given; because that Jesus was not yet glorified.

115. John 14:17. Even the Spirit of truth; whom the world cannot receive, because it seeth him not, neither knoweth him: but ye know him; for he dwelleth with you, and shall be in you.

116. John 14:26. But the Comforter, which is the Holy Ghost, whom the Father will send in my name, he shall teach you all things, and bring all things to your remembrance, whatsoever I have said unto you.

117. John 15:26. But when the Comforter is come, whom I will send unto you from the Father, even the Spirit of truth, which proceedeth from the Father, he shall testify of me.

118. John 16:13. Howbeit when he, the Spirit of truth, is come, he will guide you into all truth: for he shall not speak of himself; but whatsoever he shall hear, that shall he speak: and he will shew you things to come.

119. John 20:22. And when he had said this, he breathed on them, and saith unto them, Receive ye the Holy Ghost.

120. Acts 1:2. Until the day in which he was taken up, after that he through the Holy Ghost had given commandments unto the apostles whom he had chosen.
121. Acts 1:5. For John truly baptized with water; but ye shall be baptized with the Holy Ghost not many days hence.
122. Acts 1:8. But ye shall receive power, after that the Holy Ghost is come upon you: and ye shall be witnesses unto me both in Jerusalem, and in all Judaea, and in Samaria, and unto the uttermost part of the earth.
123. Acts 1:16. Men and brethren, this scripture must needs have been fulfilled, which the Holy Ghost by the mouth of David spake before concerning Judas, which was guide to them that took Jesus.
124. Acts 2:4. And they were all filled with the Holy Ghost, and began to speak with other tongues, as the Spirit gave them utterance.
125. Acts 2:17-18. And it shall come to pass in the last days, saith God, I will pour out of my Spirit upon all flesh: and your sons and your daughters shall prophesy, and your young men shall see visions, and your old men shall dream dreams: And on my servants and on my handmaidens I will pour out in those days of my Spirit: and they shall prophesy.
126. Acts 2:33. Therefore being by the right hand of God exalted, and having received of the Father the promise of the Holy Ghost, he hath shed forth this, which ye now see and hear.
127. Acts 2:38. Then Peter said unto them, Repent, and be baptized every one of you in the name of Jesus Christ for the remission of sins, and ye shall receive the gift of the Holy Ghost.
128. Acts 4:8. Then Peter, filled with the Holy Ghost, said unto them, Ye rulers of the people, and elders of Israel.
129. Acts 4:31. And when they had prayed, the place was shaken where they were assembled together; and they were all filled with the Holy Ghost, and they spake the word of God with boldness.
130. Acts 5:3. But Peter said, Ananias, why hath Satan filled thine heart to lie to the Holy Ghost, and to keep back part of the price of the land?
131. Acts 5:9. Then Peter said unto her, How is it that ye have agreed together to tempt the Spirit of the Lord? behold, the feet of them which have buried thy husband are at the door, and shall carry thee out.
132. Acts 5:32. And we are his witnesses of these things; and so is also the Holy Ghost, whom God hath given to them that obey him.
133. Acts 6:3. Wherefore, brethren, look ye out among you seven men of honest report, full of the Holy Ghost and wisdom, whom we may appoint over this business.
134. Acts 6:5. And the saying pleased the whole multitude: and they chose Stephen, a man full of faith and of the Holy Ghost, and Philip, and Prochorus, and Nicanor, and Timon, and Parmenas, and Nicolas a proselyte of Antioch.

135. Acts 7:51. Ye stiffnecked and uncircumcised in heart and ears, ye do always resist the Holy Ghost: as your fathers did, so do ye.

136. Acts 7:55. But he, being full of the Holy Ghost, looked up stedfastly into heaven, and saw the glory of God, and Jesus standing on the right hand of God.

137. Acts 8:15. Who, when they were come down, prayed for them, that they might receive the Holy Ghost.

138. Acts 8:17-19. Then laid they their hands on them, and they received the Holy Ghost. And when Simon saw that through laying on of the apostles' hands the Holy Ghost was given, he offered them money. Saying, Give me also this power, that on whomsoever I lay hands, he may receive the Holy Ghost.

139. Acts 8:29. Then the Spirit said unto Philip, Go near, and join thyself to this chariot.

140. Acts 8:39. And when they were come up out of the water, the Spirit of the Lord caught away Philip, that the eunuch saw him no more: and he went on his way rejoicing.

141. Acts 9:17. And Ananias went his way, and entered into the house; and putting his hands on him said, Brother Saul, the Lord, even Jesus, that appeared unto thee in the way as thou camest, hath sent me, that thou mightest receive thy sight, and be filled with the Holy Ghost.

142. Acts 9:31. Then had the churches rest throughout all Judaea and Galilee and Samaria, and were edified; and walking in the fear of the Lord, and in the comfort of the Holy Ghost, were multiplied.

143. Acts 10:19. While Peter thought on the vision, the Spirit said unto him, Behold, three men seek thee.

144. Acts 10:38. How God anointed Jesus of Nazareth with the Holy Ghost and with power: who went about doing good, and healing all that were oppressed of the devil; for God was with him.

145. Acts 10:44-45. While Peter yet spake these words, the Holy Ghost fell on all them which heard the word. And they of the circumcision which believed were astonished, as many as came with Peter, because that on the Gentiles also was poured out the gift of the Holy Ghost.

146. Acts 10:47. Can any man forbid water, that these should not be baptized, which have received the Holy Ghost as well as we?

147. Acts 11:12. And the spirit bade me go with them, nothing doubting. Moreover these six brethren accompanied me, and we entered into the man's house.

148. Acts 11:15-16. And as I began to speak, the Holy Ghost fell on them, as on us at the beginning. Then remembered I the word of the Lord, how that he said, John indeed baptized with water; but ye shall be baptized with the Holy Ghost.

149. Acts 11:24. For he was a good man, and full of the Holy Ghost and of faith: and much people was added unto the Lord.

150. Acts 11:28. And there stood up one of them named Agabus, and signified by the spirit that there should be great dearth throughout all the world: which came to pass in the days of Claudius Caesar.
151. Acts 13:2. As they ministered to the Lord, and fasted, the Holy Ghost said, Separate me Barnabas and Saul for the work whereunto I have called them.
152. Acts 13:4. So they, being sent forth by the Holy Ghost, departed unto Seleucia; and from thence they sailed to Cyprus.
153. Acts 13:9. Then Saul, (who also is called Paul,) filled with the Holy Ghost, set his eyes on him.
154. Acts 13:52. And the disciples were filled with joy, and with the Holy Ghost.
155. Acts 15:8. And God, which knoweth the hearts, bare them witness, giving them the Holy Ghost, even as he did unto us.
156. Acts 15:28. For it seemed good to the Holy Ghost, and to us, to lay upon you no greater burden than these necessary things.
157. Acts 16:6-7. Now when they had gone throughout Phrygia and the region of Galatia, and were forbidden of the Holy Ghost to preach the word in Asia, After they were come to Mysia, they assayed to go into Bithynia: but the Spirit suffered them not.
158. Acts 19:2. He said unto them, Have ye received the Holy Ghost since ye believed? And they said unto him, We have not so much as heard whether there be any Holy Ghost.
159. Acts 19:6. And when Paul had laid his hands upon them, the Holy Ghost came on them; and they spake with tongues, and prophesied.
160. Acts 20:28. Take heed therefore unto yourselves, and to all the flock, over the which the Holy Ghost hath made you overseers, to feed the church of God, which he hath purchased with his own blood.
161. Acts 21:4. And finding disciples, we tarried there seven days: who said to Paul through the Spirit, that he should not go up to Jerusalem.
162. Acts 21:11. And when he was come unto us, he took Paul's girdle, and bound his own hands and feet, and said, Thus saith the Holy Ghost, So shall the Jews at Jerusalem bind the man that owneth this girdle, and shall deliver him into the hands of the Gentiles.
163. Acts 23:8-9. For the Sadducees say that there is no resurrection, neither angel, nor spirit: but the Pharisees confess both. And there arose a great cry: and the scribes that were of the Pharisees' part arose, and strove, saying, We find no evil in this man: but if a spirit or an angel hath spoken to him, let us not fight against God.
164. Acts 28:25. And when they agreed not among themselves, they departed, after that Paul had spoken one word, Well spake the Holy Ghost by Esaias the prophet unto our fathers.
165. Romans 1:4. And declared to be the Son of God with power, according to the spirit of holiness, by the resurrection from the dead.

166. Romans 5:5. And hope maketh not ashamed; because the love of God is shed abroad in our hearts by the Holy Ghost which is given unto us.

167. Romans 8:1-2. There is therefore now no condemnation to them which are in Christ Jesus, who walk not after the flesh, but after the Spirit. For the law of the Spirit of life in Christ Jesus hath made me free from the law of sin and death.

168. Romans 8:4-5. That the righteousness of the law might be fulfilled in us, who walk not after the flesh, but after the Spirit. For they that are after the flesh do mind the things of the flesh; but they that are after the Spirit the things of the Spirit.

169. Romans 8:9-11. But ye are not in the flesh, but in the Spirit, if so be that the Spirit of God dwell in you. Now if any man have not the Spirit of Christ, he is none of his. And if Christ be in you, the body is dead because of sin; but the Spirit is life because of righteousness. But if the Spirit of him that raised up Jesus from the dead dwell in you, he that raised up Christ from the dead shall also quicken your mortal bodies by his Spirit that dwelleth in you.

170. Romans 8:13-16. For if ye live after the flesh, ye shall die: but if ye through the Spirit do mortify the deeds of the body, ye shall live. For as many as are led by the Spirit of God, they are the sons of God. For ye have not received the spirit of bondage again to fear; but ye have received the Spirit of adoption, whereby we cry, Abba, Father. The Spirit itself beareth witness with our spirit, that we are the children of God.

171. Romans 8:23. And not only they, but ourselves also, which have the firstfruits of the Spirit, even we ourselves groan within ourselves, waiting for the adoption, to wit, the redemption of our body.

172. Romans 8:26-27. Likewise the Spirit also helpeth our infirmities: for we know not what we should pray for as we ought: but the Spirit itself maketh intercession for us with groanings which cannot be uttered. And he that searcheth the hearts knoweth what is the mind of the Spirit, because he maketh intercession for the saints according to the will of God.

173. Romans 9:1. I say the truth in Christ, I lie not, my conscience also bearing me witness in the Holy Ghost.

174. Romans 14:17. For the kingdom of God is not meat and drink; but righteousness, and peace, and joy in the Holy Ghost.

175. Romans 15:13. Now the God of hope fill you with all joy and peace in believing, that ye may abound in hope, through the power of the Holy Ghost.

176. Romans 15:16. That I should be the minister of Jesus Christ to the Gentiles, ministering the gospel of God, that the offering up of the Gentiles might be acceptable, being sanctified by the Holy Ghost.

177. Romans 15:19. Through mighty signs and wonders, by the power of the Spirit of God; so that from Jerusalem, and round about unto Illyricum, I have fully preached the gospel of Christ.

178. Romans 15:30. Now I beseech you, brethren, for the Lord Jesus Christ's sake, and for the love of the Spirit, that ye strive together with me in your prayers to God for me.

179. 1 Corinthians 2:4. And my speech and my preaching was not with enticing words of man's wisdom, but in demonstration of the Spirit and of power.

180. 1 Corinthians 2:10-14 But God hath revealed them unto us by his Spirit: for the Spirit searcheth all things, yea, the deep things of God. For what man knoweth the things of a man, save the spirit of man which is in him? even so the things of God knoweth no man, but the Spirit of God. Now we have received, not the spirit of the world, but the spirit which is of God; that we might know the things that are freely given to us of God. Which things also we speak, not in the words which man's wisdom teacheth, but which the Holy Ghost teacheth; comparing spiritual things with spiritual. But the natural man receiveth not the things of the Spirit of God: for they are foolishness unto him: neither can he know them, because they are spiritually discerned.

181. 1 Corinthians 3:16. Know ye not that ye are the temple of God, and that the Spirit of God dwelleth in you?

182. 1 Corinthians 6:11. And such were some of you: but ye are washed, but ye are sanctified, but ye are justified in the name of the Lord Jesus, and by the Spirit of our God.

183. 1 Corinthians 6:17. But he that is joined unto the Lord is one spirit.

184. 1 Corinthians 6:19. What? know ye not that your body is the temple of the Holy Ghost which is in you, which ye have of God, and ye are not your own?

185. 1 Corinthians 7:40. But she is happier if she so abide, after my judgment: and I think also that I have the Spirit of God.

186. 1 Corinthians 12:3. Wherefore I give you to understand, that no man speaking by the Spirit of God calleth Jesus accursed: and that no man can say that Jesus is the Lord, but by the Holy Ghost.

187. 1 Corinthians 12:4. Now there are diversities of gifts, but the same Spirit.

188. 1 Corinthians 12:7. But the manifestation of the Spirit is given to every man to profit withal.

189. 1 Corinthians 12:8-9 For to one is given by the Spirit the word of wisdom; to another the word of knowledge by the same Spirit; To another faith by the same Spirit; to another the gifts of healing by the same Spirit.

190. 1 Corinthians 12:11. But all these worketh that one and the selfsame Spirit, dividing to every man severally as he will.

191. 1 Corinthians 12:13. For by one Spirit are we all baptized into one body, whether we be Jews or Gentiles, whether we be bond or free; and have been all made to drink into one Spirit.

192. 1 Corinthians 14:2. For he that speaketh in an unknown tongue speaketh not unto men, but unto God: for no man understandeth him; howbeit in the spirit he speaketh mysteries.

193. 1 Corinthians 14:14-16 For if I pray in an unknown tongue, my spirit prayeth, but my understanding is unfruitful. What is it then? I will pray with the spirit, and I will pray with the understanding also: I will sing with the spirit, and I will sing with the understanding also. Else when thou shalt bless with the spirit, how shall he that occupieth the room of the unlearned say Amen at thy giving of thanks, seeing he understandeth not what thou sayest?

194. 1 Corinthians 15:45. And so it is written, The first man Adam was made a living soul; the last Adam was made a quickening spirit.

195. 2 Corinthians 1:22. Who hath also sealed us, and given the earnest of the Spirit in our hearts.

196. 2 Corinthians 3:3. Forasmuch as ye are manifestly declared to be the epistle of Christ ministered by us, written not with ink, but with the Spirit of the living God; not in tables of stone, but in fleshy tables of the heart.

197. 2 Corinthians 3:6. Who also hath made us able ministers of the new testament; not of the letter, but of the spirit: for the letter killeth, but the spirit giveth life.

198. 2 Corinthians 3:8. How shall not the ministration of the spirit be rather glorious?

199. 2 Corinthians 3:17-18. Now the Lord is that Spirit: and where the Spirit of the Lord is, there is liberty. But we all, with open face beholding as in a glass the glory of the Lord, are changed into the same image from glory to glory, even as by the Spirit of the Lord.

200. 2 Corinthians 5:5. Now he that hath wrought us for the selfsame thing is God, who also hath given unto us the earnest of the Spirit. NLT. God himself has prepared us for this, and as a guarantee he has given us his Holy Spirit.

201. 2 Corinthians 6:6. By pureness, by knowledge, by longsuffering, by kindness, by the Holy Ghost, by love unfeigned.

202. 2 Corinthians 13:14. The grace of the Lord Jesus Christ, and the love of God, and the communion of the Holy Ghost, be with you all. Amen.

203. Galatians 3:2-3. This only would I learn of you, Received ye the Spirit by the works of the law, or by the hearing of faith? Are ye so foolish? having begun in the Spirit, are ye now made perfect by the flesh?

204. Galatians 3:5. He therefore that ministereth to you the Spirit, and worketh miracles among you, doeth he it by the works of the law, or by the hearing of faith?

205. Galatians 3:14. That the blessing of Abraham might come on the Gentiles through Jesus Christ; that we might receive the promise of the Spirit through faith.

206. Galatians 4:6. And because ye are sons, God hath sent forth the Spirit of his Son into your hearts, crying, Abba, Father.

207. Galatians 4:29. But as then he that was born after the flesh persecuted him that was born after the Spirit, even so it is now.

208. Galatians 5:5. For we through the Spirit wait for the hope of righteousness by faith.

209. Galatians 5:16-18. This I say then, Walk in the Spirit, and ye shall not fulfil the lust of the flesh. For the flesh lusteth against the Spirit, and the Spirit against the flesh: and these are contrary the one to the other: so that ye cannot do the things that ye would. But if ye be led of the Spirit, ye are not under the law.

210. Galatians 5:22-23. But the fruit of the Spirit is love, joy, peace, longsuffering, gentleness, goodness, faith, meekness, temperance: against such there is no law.

211. Galatians 5:25. If we live in the Spirit, let us also walk in the Spirit.

212. Galatians 6:8. For he that soweth to his flesh shall of the flesh reap corruption; but he that soweth to the Spirit shall of the Spirit reap life everlasting.

213. Ephesians 1:13. In whom ye also trusted, after that ye heard the word of truth, the gospel of your salvation: in whom also after that ye believed, ye were sealed with that holy Spirit of promise.

214. Ephesians 1:17. That the God of our Lord Jesus Christ, the Father of glory, may give unto you the spirit of wisdom and revelation in the knowledge of him.

215. Ephesians 2:18. For through him we both have access by one Spirit unto the Father.

216. Ephesians 2:22. In whom ye also are builded together for an habitation of God through the Spirit.

217. Ephesians 3:5. Which in other ages was not made known unto the sons of men, as it is now revealed unto his holy apostles and prophets by the Spirit.

218. Ephesians 3:16. That he would grant you, according to the riches of his glory, to be strengthened with might by his Spirit in the inner man.

219. Ephesians 4:3-4 Endeavouring to keep the unity of the Spirit in the bond of peace. There is one body, and one Spirit, even as ye are called in one hope of your calling.

220. Ephesians 4:30. And grieve not the holy Spirit of God, whereby ye are sealed unto the day of redemption.

221. Ephesians 5:9. (For the fruit of the Spirit is in all goodness and righteousness and truth.)

222. Ephesians 5:18. And be not drunk with wine, wherein is excess; but be filled with the Spirit.

223. Ephesians 6:17. And take the helmet of salvation, and the sword of the Spirit, which is the word of God.
224. Ephesians 6:18. Praying always with all prayer and supplication in the Spirit, and watching thereunto with all perseverance and supplication for all saints.
225. Philippians 1:27. Only let your conversation be as it becometh the gospel of Christ: that whether I come and see you, or else be absent, I may hear of your affairs, that ye stand fast in one spirit, with one mind striving together for the faith of the gospel.
226. Philippians 2:1. If there be therefore any consolation in Christ, if any comfort of love, if any fellowship of the Spirit, if any bowels and mercies. NLT. Is there any encouragement from belonging to Christ? Any comfort from his love? Any fellowship together in the Spirit? Are your hearts tender and compassionate?
227. Philippians 3:3. For we are the circumcision, which worship God in the spirit, and rejoice in Christ Jesus, and have no confidence in the flesh. NLT. For we who worship by the Spirit of God are the ones who are truly circumcised. We rely on what Christ Jesus has done for us. We put no confidence in human effort.
228. Colossians 1:8. Who also declared unto us your love in the Spirit.
229. Colossians 2:5. For though I be absent in the flesh, yet am I with you in the spirit, joying and beholding your order, and the stedfastness of your faith in Christ.
230. 1 Thessalonians 1:5-6 For our gospel came not unto you in word only, but also in power, and in the Holy Ghost, and in much assurance; as ye know what manner of men we were among you for your sake. And ye became followers of us, and of the Lord, having received the word in much affliction, with joy of the Holy Ghost.
231. 1 Thessalonians 4:8. He therefore that despiseth, despiseth not man, but God, who hath also given unto us his holy Spirit.
232. 1 Thessalonians 5:19. Quench not the Spirit.
233. 2 Thessalonians 2:8. And then shall that Wicked be revealed, whom the Lord shall consume with the spirit of his mouth, and shall destroy with the brightness of his coming.
234. 2 Thessalonians 2:13. But we are bound to give thanks alway to God for you, brethren beloved of the Lord, because God hath from the beginning chosen you to salvation through sanctification of the Spirit and belief of the truth.
235. 1 Timothy 3:16. And without controversy great is the mystery of godliness: God was manifest in the flesh, justified in the Spirit, seen of angels, preached unto the Gentiles, believed on in the world, received up into glory.
236. 1 Timothy 4:1. Now the Spirit speaketh expressly, that in the latter times some shall depart from the faith, giving heed to seducing spirits, and doctrines of devils.

237. 2 Timothy 1:14. That good thing which was committed unto thee keep by the Holy Ghost which dwelleth in us.

238. Titus 3:5. Not by works of righteousness which we have done, but according to his mercy he saved us, by the washing of regeneration, and renewing of the Holy Ghost,

239. Hebrews 2:3-4. How shall we escape, if we neglect so great salvation; which at the first began to be spoken by the Lord, and was confirmed unto us by them that heard him; God also bearing them witness, both with signs and wonders, and with divers miracles, and gifts of the Holy Ghost, according to his own will?

240. Hebrews 3:7-8. Wherefore (as the Holy Ghost saith, To day if ye will hear his voice, Harden not your hearts, as in the provocation, in the day of temptation in the wilderness.

241. Hebrews 6:4-6. For it is impossible for those who were once enlightened, and have tasted of the heavenly gift, and were made partakers of the Holy Ghost, And have tasted the good word of God, and the powers of the world to come, If they shall fall away, to renew them again unto repentance; seeing they crucify to themselves the Son of God afresh, and put him to an open shame.

242. Hebrews 9:8. The Holy Ghost this signifying, that the way into the holiest of all was not yet made manifest, while as the first tabernacle was yet standing.

243. Hebrews 9:14-15. How much more shall the blood of Christ, who through the eternal Spirit offered himself without spot to God, purge your conscience from dead works to serve the living God? Whereof the Holy Ghost also is a witness to us.

244. Hebrews 10:29. Of how much sorer punishment, suppose ye, shall he be thought worthy, who hath trodden under foot the Son of God, and hath counted the blood of the covenant, wherewith he was sanctified, an unholy thing, and hath done despite unto the Spirit of grace?
NLT. Just think how much worse the punishment will be for those who have trampled on the Son of God, and have treated the blood of the covenant, which made us holy, as if it were common and unholy, and have insulted and disdained the Holy Spirit who brings God's mercy to us.

James 4:5. Do ye think that the scripture saith in vain, The spirit that dwelleth in us lusteth to envy?
NLT. What do you think the Scriptures mean when they say that the spirit God has placed within us is filled with envy?

245. 1 Peter 1:2. Elect according to the foreknowledge of God the Father, through sanctification of the Spirit, unto obedience and sprinkling of the blood of Jesus Christ: Grace unto you, and peace, be multiplied.

246. 1 Peter 1:11-12. Searching what, or what manner of time the Spirit of Christ which was in them did signify, when it testified beforehand the sufferings of Christ, and the glory that should follow. Unto whom it was revealed, that not unto themselves, but unto us they did minister the things, which are now reported unto you by them that have preached the gospel unto you with the Holy Ghost sent down from heaven; which things the angels desire to look into.

247. 1 Peter 1:22. Seeing ye have purified your souls in obeying the truth through the Spirit unto unfeigned love of the brethren, see that ye love one another with a pure heart fervently.

248. 1 Peter 3:18. For Christ also hath once suffered for sins, the just for the unjust, that he might bring us to God, being put to death in the flesh, but quickened by the Spirit.

249. 1 Peter 4:14. If ye be reproached for the name of Christ, happy are ye; for the spirit of glory and of God resteth upon you: on their part he is evil spoken of, but on your part he is glorified.

250. 2 Peter 1:21. For the prophecy came not in old time by the will of man: but holy men of God spake as they were moved by the Holy Ghost.

251. 1 John 3:24. And he that keepeth his commandments dwelleth in him, and he in him. And hereby we know that he abideth in us, by the Spirit which he hath given us.

252. 1 John 4:1-3. Beloved, believe not every spirit, but try the spirits whether they are of God: because many false prophets are gone out into the world. Hereby know ye the Spirit of God: Every spirit that confesseth that Jesus Christ is come in the flesh is of God: And every spirit that confesseth not that Jesus Christ is come in the flesh is not of God: and this is that spirit of antichrist, whereof ye have heard that it should come; and even now already is it in the world.

253. 1 John 4:6. We are of God: he that knoweth God heareth us; he that is not of God heareth not us. Hereby know we the spirit of truth, and the spirit of error.

254. 1 John 4:13. Hereby know we that we dwell in him, and he in us, because he hath given us of his Spirit.

255. 1 John 5:6-8. This is he that came by water and blood, even Jesus Christ; not by water only, but by water and blood. And it is the Spirit that beareth witness, because the Spirit is truth. For there are three that bear record in heaven, the Father, the Word, and the Holy Ghost: and these three are one. And there are three that bear witness in earth, the spirit, and the water, and the blood: and these three agree in one.

256. Jude 19-21. These be they who separate themselves, sensual, having not the Spirit, But ye, beloved, building up yourselves on your most holy faith, praying in the Holy Ghost, Keep yourselves in the love of God, looking for the mercy of our Lord Jesus Christ unto eternal life.

257. Revelation 1:10. I was in the Spirit on the Lord's day, and heard behind me a great voice, as of a trumpet.

258. Revelation 2:7. He that hath an ear, let him hear what the Spirit saith unto the churches: To him that overcometh will I give to eat of the tree of life, which is in the midst of the paradise of God.

259. Revelation 2:11. He that hath an ear, let him hear what the Spirit saith unto the churches: He that overcometh shall not be hurt of the second death.

260. Revelation 2:17. He that hath an ear, let him hear what the Spirit saith unto the churches: To him that overcometh will I give to eat of the hidden manna, and will give him a white stone, and in the stone a new name written, which no man knoweth saving he that receiveth it.

261. Revelation 2:29. He that hath an ear, let him hear what the Spirit saith unto the churches.

262. Revelation 3:6. He that hath an ear, let him hear what the Spirit saith unto the churches.

263. Revelation 3:13. He that hath an ear, let him hear what the Spirit saith unto the churches.

264. Revelation 3:22. He that hath an ear, let him hear what the Spirit saith unto the churches.

265. Revelation 4:2. And immediately I was in the spirit: and, behold, a throne was set in heaven, and one sat on the throne.

266. Revelation 11:11. And after three days and an half the Spirit of life from God entered into them, and they stood upon their feet; and great fear fell upon them which saw them.

267. Revelation 14:13. And I heard a voice from heaven saying unto me, Write, Blessed are the dead which die in the Lord from henceforth: Yea, saith the Spirit, that they may rest from their labours; and their works do follow them.

268. Revelation 17:3. So he carried me away in the spirit into the wilderness: and I saw a woman sit upon a scarlet coloured beast, full of names of blasphemy, having seven heads and ten horns.

269. Revelation 21:10. And he carried me away in the spirit to a great and high mountain, and shewed me that great city, the holy Jerusalem, descending out of heaven from God.

270. Revelation 22:17. And the Spirit and the bride say, Come. And let him that heareth say, Come. And let him that is athirst come. And whosoever will, let him take the water of life freely.

APPENDIX 2

HISTORICAL CREEDS HONORING MY FRIEND

Throughout the history of the Christian Church, battles have been fought not only over the deity of Jesus but also over the deity of the Holy Ghost. In this section are excerpts from historical Christian documents affirming that Jesus is God and Holy Ghost is God.

THE CHICAGO STATEMENT ON BIBLICAL INERRANCY[6]

1. God, who is Himself Truth and speaks truth only, has inspired Holy Scripture in order thereby to reveal Himself to lost mankind through Jesus Christ as Creator and Lord, Redeemer and Judge. Holy Scripture is God's witness to Himself.

2. Holy Scripture, being God's own Word, written by men prepared and superintended by His Spirit, is of infallible divine authority in all matters upon which it touches: it is to be believed, as God's instruction, in all that it affirms, obeyed, as God's command, in all that it requires; embraced, as God's pledge, in all that it promises.

3. The Holy Spirit, Scripture's divine Author, both authenticates it to us by His inward witness and opens our minds to understand its meaning.

4. Being wholly and verbally God-given, Scripture is without error or fault in all its teaching, no less in what it states about God's acts in creation,

---

[6] Excerpt. Created in 1978 at a gathering of Christian leaders. Available online at http://www.reformation.net/COR/cordocs/inerrancy.pdf.

about the events of world history, and about its own literary origins under God, than in its witness to God's saving grace in individual lives.

5. The authority of Scripture is inescapably impaired if this total divine inerrancy is in any way limited or disregarded, or made relative to a view of truth contrary to the Bible's own; and such lapses bring serious loss to both the individual and the Church.

THE NICENE CREED AND THE HOLY GHOST

The Nicene Creed was written in 325 A.D. at the time of an unbelievable breakthrough of the Holy Ghost, the Spirit of Truth, in correcting church doctrine. For the first time a Roman emperor, Constantine, was not persecuting the church but endorsing it. And it was Constantine who called together approximately 300 bishops and deacons to stop their disagreements among themselves and create a common creed.

Converted to Christianity in 312 just before a decisive battle, Constantine said at the Council of Nicea, "Division in the church is worse than war." In future years, Constantine would become less interested in strict orthodoxy, and turn against Athanasius, the bishop of Alexandria, for maintaining his unwavering position on truth, but that one Council of Nicaea had such an impact that we still appreciate the results today.

Athanasius confronts the Arian heresy

The Council of Nicaea dealt explicitly with the heretical position promoted by Arius, an influential pastor in Alexandria, Egypt, that Christ was not fully God. He said that Christ was created by God and in turn Christ created everything else. Christ was neither equal nor co-eternal with the Father. He was a sort of demigod—supernatural, but not quite human or divine. The strongest voice opposing him on behalf of biblical orthodoxy was Athanasius, then a deacon from Alexandria.

Athanasius

Athanasius of Alexandria was an Egyptian church leader of the fourth century who at the age of 27 took a distinctly biblical stand at the Council of Nicaea against the heresy of Arius and Arianism which said that Christ was of a different substance from the Father. Three years later he became archbishop of Alexandria.

For the rest of his life he stood boldly against the Arians and later against the Emperor Constantine even though he was several times forced into exile. His writings are still respected for their orthodoxy.

226

Future Nicene Creed revisions include more on the Holy Ghost

The Nicene Creed was changed a few more times to continue to address heresy. In the 9th century, the Western church added a phrase that is called "The Filioque" from the Latin word meaning "and the Son." With this addition, it reads, "And in the Holy Ghost . . . Who proceedeth from the Father and the Son *(Latin: qui ex Patre Filioque procedit).*

The Nicene Creed is the official creed of the Roman Catholic, Orthodox, and some Protestant churches.

TEXT OF THE MODERN NICENE CREED

I believe in one God the Father Almighty, maker of heaven and earth, and of all things visible and invisible:

And in one Lord Jesus Christ, the only-begotten Son of God, begotten of the Father before all worlds, God of God, Light of Light, very God of very God; begotten, not made, being of one substance with the Father by whom all things were made, who for us men and for our salvation came down from heaven, and was incarnate by the Holy Ghost of the Virgin Mary, and was made man, and was crucified also for us under Pontius Pilate. He suffered and was buried, and the third day he rose again according to the Scriptures and ascended into heaven, and sitteth on the right hand of the Father; and he shall come again, with glory, to judge both the quick and the dead whose kingdom shall have no end:

And I believe in the Holy Ghost, the Lord, and Giver of life, who proceedeth from the Father and the Son, who with Father and Son together is worshipped and glorified, who spake by the prophets. And I believe in one holy catholic and Apostolic Church; I acknowledge one baptism for the remission of sins, and I look for the resurrection of the dead, and the life of the world to come. Amen.

THE APOSTLES' CREED

The creed that is called "The Apostles' Creed" is the oldest creed. Even though it is not considered the work of the original apostles, it dates to those times and held a respected place in the early church.[7]

TEXT OF THE APOSTLES' CREED

I believe in God the Father Almighty, Maker of heaven and earth. And in Jesus Christ his only Son our Lord; who was conceived by the Holy Ghost, born of the Virgin Mary, suffered under Pontius Pilate, was crucified, dead, and buried; he descended into hell; the third day he rose again from the dead; he ascended into heaven, and sitteth on the right hand of God the Father Almighty; from thence he shall come to judge the quick and the dead. I believe in the Holy Ghost; the holy catholic Church; the communion of saints; the forgiveness of sins; the resurrection of the body; and the life everlasting. Amen.

THE WESTMINSTER SHORTER CATECHISM[8]

Question 1. What is the chief end of man?
Answer 1. Man's chief end is to glorify God, and to enjoy Him for ever.

Question 2. What rule hath God given to direct us how we may glorify and enjoy Him?
Answer 2. The Word of God, which is contained in the Scriptures of the Old and New Testaments, is the only rule to direct us how we may glorify and enjoy Him.

Question 3. What do the Scriptures principally teach?
Answer 3. The Scriptures principally teach what man is to believe concerning God, and what duty God requires of man.

Question 4. What is God?
Answer 4. God is a Spirit, infinite, eternal, and unchangeable, in his being, wisdom, power, holiness, justice, goodness, and truth.

---

[7] International Standard Bible Encyclopedia. Online at http://topicalbible.org/c/creed.htm
[8] This is an excerpt. Additional questions can be found online at several sites, including http://bible.crosswalk.com/History/AD/CreedsandConfessions/Catechisms/TheWestminsterCatechism_Shorter.html. Crosswalk.com also provides many other resources.

Question 5. Are there more Gods than one?
Answer 5. There is but one only, the living and true God.

Question 6. How many persons are there in the Godhead?
Answer 6. There are three persons in the Godhead; the Father, the Son, and the Holy Ghost, and these three are one God, the same in substance, equal in power and glory.

Question 7. What are the decrees of God?
Answer 7. The decrees of God are, his eternal purpose, according to the counsel of his will, whereby, for his own glory, he hath fore-ordained whatsoever comes to pass.

Question 8. How doth God execute his decrees?
Answer 8. God executeth his decrees in the works of creation and providence.

Question 9. What is the work of creation?
Answer 9. The work of creation is, God's making all things of nothing, by the word of his power, in the space of six days, and all very good.

Question 10. How did God create man?
Answer 10. God created man male and female, after his own image, in knowledge, righteousness, and holiness, with dominion over the creatures.

Question 11. What are God's works of providence?
Answer 11. God's works of providence are, his most holy, wise, and powerful preserving and governing all his creatures, and all their actions.

Question 12. What special act of providence did God exercise toward man in the estate wherein he was created?
Answer 12. When God had created man, he entered into a covenant of life with him, upon condition of perfect obedience; forbidding him to eat of the tree of the knowledge of good and evil, upon the pain of death.

Question 13. Did our first parents continue in the estate wherein they were created?
Answer 13. Our first parents, being left to the freedom of their own will, fell from the estate wherein they were created, by sinning against God.

Question 14. What is sin?
Answer 14. Sin is any want of conformity unto, or transgression of, the law of God.

Question 15. What was the sin whereby our first parents fell from the estate wherein they were created?
Answer 15. The sin whereby our first parents fell from the estate wherein they were created was their eating the forbidden fruit.

Question 16. Did all mankind fall in Adam's first transgression?
Answer 16. The covenant being made with Adam, not only for himself, but for his posterity; all mankind, descending from him by ordinary generation, sinned in him, and fell with him, in his first transgression.

Question 17. Into what estate did the fall bring mankind?
Answer 17. The fall brought mankind into an estate of sin and misery.
Question 18. Wherein consists the sinfulness of that estate whereinto man fell?
Answer 18. The sinfulness of that estate whereinto man fell, consists in the guilt of Adam's first sin, the want of original righteousness, and the corruption of his whole nature, which is commonly called Original Sin; together with all actual transgressions which proceed from it.

Question 19. What is the misery of that estate whereinto man fell?
Answer 19. All mankind by their fall lost communion with God, are under his wrath and curse, and so made liable to all miseries in this life, to death itself, and to the pains of hell for ever.

Question 20. Did God leave all mankind to perish in the estate of sin and misery?
Answer 20. God having, out of his mere good pleasure, from all eternity, elected some to everlasting life, did enter into a covenant of grace, to deliver them out of the estate of sin and misery, and to bring them into an estate of salvation by a Redeemer.

Question 21. Who is the Redeemer of God's elect?
Answer 21. The only Redeemer of God's elect is the Lord Jesus Christ.[9]

---

[9] Additional questions and answers can be found online at several sites, including http://bible.crosswalk.com/History/AD/CreedsandConfessions/Catechisms/TheWestminsterCatechism_Shorter.html. Crosswalk.com also provides many other resources.

BISHOP WELLINGTON BOONE serves his congregation, The Father's House, in Norcross, Georgia, as senior pastor and bishop. He is the founding bishop and chief prelate of the Fellowship of International Churches.

He is an author and speaker for CBN, TBN, Daystar, Promise Keepers, Focus on the Family, Men at the Cross, Salvation Army, Church of God in Christ, Family Research Council, Assemblies of God, Southern Baptist Convention, Campus Crusade, Christ for the Nations, MorningStar Ministries, and many other churches and ministries.

Regent University in 2010 received the donation of the Wellington Boone Collection into the Regent University Library. He is a former member of the Board of Regent University, March for Jesus, and the Evangelical Council for Financial Accountability. He currently serves on the boards of major churches and international ministries.

Bishop Boone believes in personal consecration, lifelong marriage between a man and a woman, and biblical unity in the Church. He lives out his message of humility and Christ-like servanthood with his wife of 38 years, and his family.

Life Themes of Bishop Wellington Boone
- Celebrating Families
- Training Leaders
- Reaching the World

Wellington Boone Ministries and The Father's House
5875 Peachtree Industrial Blvd., Suite 300
Norcross, Georgia 30092
770-840-0888

Wellington Boone Ministries: www.WellingtonBoone.com
The Father's House Church: www.TheFathersHouse.cc
Product Resources: www.shop.apptepublishing.com

NOTES TO MY FRIEND

NOTES TO MY FRIEND